The "Supreme Gentleman" Killer

Brian Whitney

WILDBLUE
PRESS

WildBluePress.com

THE "SUPREME GENTLEMAN" KILLER published by:
WILDBLUE PRESS
P.O. Box 102440
Denver, Colorado 80250

WILDBLUE PRESS is registered at the U.S. Patent and Trademark Offices.

ISBN 978-1-948239-69-1 Trade Paperback
ISBN 978-1-947290-15-0 eBook

Cover design © 2020 WildBlue Press. All rights reserved.

Interior Formatting by Elijah Toten
www.totencreative.com

The "Supreme Gentleman" Killer

TABLE OF CONTENTS

AUTHOR'S NOTE

No one knew the true Elliot Rodger before his death. His parents had no idea about his real thought process. He had never been in any trouble with the law. While he did go to therapy intermittently, he lied to mental health professionals about what was really going on inside of him. He had no friends. In fact, for the last few years of his life, he didn't have any real acquaintances other than his roommates who he despised.

Therefore this book is not intended to answer the question of *why* Elliot Rodger turned out to be a mass murderer. That would be impossible to do, which of course, is the scary part of the whole thing. It would be so much easier if things like this were simple.

Rather this book is the tale of his descent into madness, which he documented through his manifesto *My Twisted World*. It is also the story of how he became thought of as a "hero" and an inspiration to men who consider themselves a part of the "Incel Revolution."

FOREWORD

ANITA DALTON, AUTHOR OF THE
FORTHCOMING BOOK *BLOOD MANIFESTO*

I have developed a certain impatience with people who dismiss Elliot Rodger's manifesto *My Twisted World* because they feel it is not a manifesto. Yes, it is a memoir, but it's my belief that most manifestos not written from a specific religious or political mindset or to promote a new religious or political mindset, are largely biographical, even if the writers had no idea they were telling their life story.

Elliot Rodger is part of a new breed of manifesto writers who came of age when confessional writing online gave everyone a platform to tell their personal story. He grew up during a time when blogging encouraged people to merge all the various identities humans construct for themselves or find assigned to them into the way that they express themselves, so rejection of, say, one's politics, was a deep rejection of the self. Go on Twitter and you see personality melt downs and people descending into wholesale character assassination hourly. In such a world, where the experience of being a human being is one of shouting one's opinion into the void, merging all that makes us human into one statement that, if rejected, can threaten our very sense of self: manifestos written by those who find themselves outsiders are going to become more and more personal.

It's bafflingly dense that so many people who look at Elliot's work don't see it as the call to arms for lonely men that it surely is. Elliot was riddled with anxiety. His manifesto is one of the most nail-biting depictions of anxiety one can read. Elliot felt as if he were an alien living among humans, like there was a sort of behavior he needed to engage in to be accepted as a human: yet, he could never figure it out. There was something deeply wrong with him, so much so, that outside of anxiety and maybe being on the autism spectrum, I can't begin to hazard a guess.

Not knowing what it was that plagued him, I've come to call that plague "the lack." Elliot Rodger and other writers of manifestos, such as Arthur Bremer, Ted Kaczynski, Valerie Solanas, and Anders Behring Breivik, all had/have the lack, a specific breakdown in their personalities and mental states that prevented them from being able to navigate the world and understand basic norms of behavior. It's not autism; it's not paranoid schizophrenia. It's not universally linked to abuse or poverty; there's no religious correlation - it's just some mysterious something they lacked. *My Twisted World* is a document discussing that lack, and that lack is the key to parsing out why so many young men feel like Elliot did - that there is literally no hope for them in this world.

I had borderline maternal rumblings reading Elliot's work. I could feel his agony. I wanted to thwomp him on the head when he engaged in all his "nice boy" whining about girls wanting thugs rather than a nice boy like him. I wanted his parents, who even in his own words were attentive, kind, and worried about him, to enforce stability in his life. No more dicking with his living quarters. Establish a stable, workable schedule for custody that gave him a sense of constancy. Stop permitting his fragile psyche dictate where he went to school. By trying to be flexible and listen to their kid, his parents exacerbated the anxiety Elliot felt. Every time he got his room changed at his father's house, every time his mother moved into a new rental property, every time he spent the weekend with a rich man his mother dated and later broke up with, every time he was forced to go to some Third World country on extended vacation without asking him first, his sense of stability took a blow, creating even more anxiety.

In many ways, the only reason his teenage manual of despair is notable is because the author wrote it in anticipation of shooting up a sorority. How many whiny paragraphs filled with teen angst exist, and how many of them are cause for alarm? Tumblr is fading in popularity, but you can find writing on that site written by Elliot's age peers that makes him seem relatively sane in comparison. What is remarkable about Elliot's manifesto is how unremarkable it really is. Lots of young men have "nice guy" syndrome, feel insecure about their looks, feel like the world is set against them. Most of them grow up. And those who don't move past this never pick up a gun. Even though it feels like we are under siege at times, an ocean of incels running down city blocks in vans and shooting kids on skateboards because they can't get a date, men like Elliot are rare. The feelings are not rare, but the actions are, and the actions seem to be linked to the lack, whatever it is.

Elliot was such an asshole, though. And sadly "asshole" isn't a medically or psychologically defined condition. He had such appealing moments. Until the very end he loved his mother deeply and appreciated the efforts she made on his behalf. He had female teachers he liked and wanted to like him, so he tried very hard to behave when in elementary school, and invariably these women rewarded his efforts. But then he downshifts into the sort of kid who throws coffee from his car at couples who upset him, who is so enraged by a blonde talking to another man in class that he storms out, refusing to attend college courses because of the seething hatred he had for women. In most young men, positive female relatives cause them to see other women as humans, with the right to shape their destinies as they see fit. No matter how much I read *My Twisted World*, I cannot find the moment when he turned the corner from the kid who loved his grandmothers to the man who declared all women as worthless whores because they wouldn't walk up to him, a stranger, and offer their eternal love the moment they saw him. And if they had, he would have run the other way, I am sure of it, because while Elliot's lack manifested in his utter rejection of women as human beings, his utter rejection of women as human beings did not cause the lack. He was terrified of life in all its many forms, and such terror would have made him suspicious or afraid of any woman who actually behaved the way he thought women should behave.

There is little use in speaking to friends and family to find answers about who Elliot truly was because while Elliot was troubled, he wasn't like Adam Lanza-level batshit. No one was surprised Lanza shot up a school. But Elliot hid his lack well enough that those close to him worried he would kill himself, not others. They had no clue he had access to guns. His YouTube videos were so bizarre they seemed comical at times, and his parents were actively getting him help, or at least they thought they were. But Peter Rodger said that Elliot was such a good liar that he had no idea what a good liar he was. And those who knew him, especially those name-dropped in the manifesto, have zero desire to keep rehashing this.

> *All I ever wanted was to love women, and in turn to be loved by them back. Their behavior towards me has only earned my hatred, and rightfully so! I am the true victim in all of this. I am the good guy. Humanity struck at me first by condemning me to experience so much suffering. I didn't ask for this. I didn't want this. I didn't start this war... I wasn't the one who struck first... But I will finish it by striking back. I will punish everyone. And it will be beautiful. Finally, at long last, I can show the world my true worth.*—Elliot Rodger

THE DAY OF RETRIBUTION

Elliot Rodger thought he looked very handsome on the morning of May 24, 2014.

In his mind, he was quite the catch. He was ridiculously intelligent and refined, with impeccable manners. On this morning, his hair looked fantastic as always, and he was dressed stylishly, wearing expensive clothes that were typically in fashion. Sure, he might be a tiny bit short, but his striking good looks more than made up for it.

So how was it he had laid in wait for his roommates, so he could kill them one by one, in an attempt to turn his apartment into a place where he could lure unsuspecting females (only the hottest ones, of course) to their deaths?

It's a long story. But the short story is, in Elliot's opinion, it certainly wasn't his fault.

It wasn't that he even wanted to kill his roommates all that much, not at all really, there was no reason to, other than they were quite annoying to him. They weren't popular, and they certainly weren't having sex with beautiful blonde women. Yet, they were irritating to Elliot, in large part because they bore witness to his misery in a way no one else in the world could. They saw what his life was truly like: they knew he was friendless, alone, a virgin.

But this was not the reason he killed them. The true reason was so he could set up a torture chamber in his apartment he shared with them, which was meant for those that he really wanted to destroy—beautiful women and the men they hung out with. It was hard to have a torture chamber when one has roommates. They might have said something, or even called the police, and ruined Elliot's plan.

The killings occurred at the Capri Apartments located on Seville Road, in the town of Isla Vista. The apartment was located close to Santa Barbara Community College. No one really knows when he slaughtered the three men. He may have even killed them on May 23, but it is thought they were killed on the twenty-fourth around three hours before he went out to kill more. Police found their bodies early in the morning of the twenty-fifth. The victims were Weihan Wang and Cheng Hong, both of them Elliot's roomies, as well as George Chen, who was their friend.

Chen was born in San Jose. His parents were both engineers. Chen wanted to be one as well; his dream was to work at Lockheed Martin. Chen was known as a very nice young man, who would often pick up elderly neighbors' mail or take out their trash. He was a practicing Buddhist.

As for Elliot's two roommates, Cheng Hong, also from San Jose, was a computer science student who grew up in Taipei. Weihan Wang was from Fremont, California. His family had emigrated from China around ten years prior to his death.

When police entered the apartment, after it all was over and Elliot was dead, the walls in the hallway near the front door were painted with blood, leading them to believe that Elliot had attacked each victim with a knife one by one as they entered. They found a towel as well as paper towels soaked with blood in the bathroom indicating Elliot had attempted to clean up the results of the carnage after each death, so the next person through his door would suspect nothing. Chen's body was found in the bathroom, while Wang and Hong's remains were placed in the bedroom that they shared. Elliot used six- to eight-inch, fixed blade hunting knives to murder the men.

Weihan Wang was the first to be killed; he was stabbed 15 times. He had numerous defensive wounds on his arms and hands. Next was Chen Hong. He had similar defensive wounds on his hands and arms and was stabbed 25 times. After they were killed, Elliot dragged them to their rooms and left them lying face down and covered them with blankets.

George Chen came in last and apparently put up a bit of a fight. He was stabbed 94 times, then was dragged to the bathroom.

Elliot Rodger, who thought of himself as "the supreme gentleman" and a man of class and taste, had waited silently for his victims to arrive. Then he slaughtered each of them with a knife, stabbing them over and over again in a manic frenzy until they were dead.

Who knows how long he sat there in wait between killings. What could possibly have been going on in his brain? Was he thrilled and excited that his Day of Retribution had finally started? Was he terrified when he realized that once he started stabbing the first victim he could never turn back again? Or was he simply out of his mind?

The bodies were covered and hidden, and he had the place to himself. It was time to start torturing people.

But obviously, he couldn't think of a good way to lure any hot girls into his new torture chamber. That must have been a rather odd moment for Elliot, sitting there in an apartment with three dead, young men, trying to figure out the next part of his plan. Elliot had never figured out how to get a woman into his apartment before, even without having all sorts of dead bodies lying around, how could he do so now?

How long did he sit in his apartment with three, fresh corpses before he went out to Starbucks around 7:30 on the evening of May 24 to buy a cup of coffee? Around 8:30 that night he sat in his car and worked on his laptop for a bit. At 9:17 he uploaded his *Day of Retribution* video to YouTube, and at 9:18 he sent his manifesto titled *My Twisted World* to about a dozen people, including his parents.

Then at around 9:27 p.m., Elliot drove his very desirable black BMW 328i, which was a gift from his mother, to the Alpha Phi sorority house at the University of California, Santa Barbara. He had sat in this car outside the sorority house many times before waiting for a beautiful woman to notice him, to engage with him, to want him somehow, but it never happened.

This time it would be different. They would notice him today. His plan was to enter the sorority and kill all of them. Some he would have to kill quickly, but others he had hoped to take his time with, to make them suffer, just as they had made him suffer his entire life.

When he got to the door it was locked. This had never occurred to him. How was he supposed to get in and slaughter them all? He knocked on the door, tentatively at first, and then a bit louder. Still, no one came. He began banging on the door, but no one arrived. Some of the sorority members who were home that night said that often people knocked on the door, but this time it was more aggressive than usual. For some reason, none of them went to see who it was. Even at the moment when his Day of Retribution was to begin, Elliot was still being ignored by women, despite his efforts to impress.

So far his Day of Retribution had only netted him three nerdy Asian men, not at all his target population of hot women and stupid jocks. Not quite what he had in mind.

He tried banging at the door a few more times, but to his great despair no one came to let him in. Elliot began to worry that he was attracting attention. He must have felt that he had no choice but to just start shooting at random people in the area, even if they weren't the hottest people he could possibly kill. This must have been irritating to him, but Elliot knew that things didn't always work out like he hoped. He would just have to start killing anyone he could, even if they were only average looking in appearance.

Elliot got back in his car.

Bianca DeKock was walking down the street with two friends, Veronica Weiss and Katherine Cooper, when she saw a man driving a BMW slowing down as he approached them. The car was moving in the same direction she and her friends were walking. She assumed the driver was looking for a place to park. She noticed the driver had his window rolled down and was alone in the vehicle. All of sudden she heard something that sounded like gunfire and felt enormous pain. She and her friends fell to the ground.

Bianca began screaming, "I'm going to die! I'm going to die!" as she lay on the sidewalk. A deputy sheriff quickly responded to the sound of gunfire and applied pressure to her wounds. She survived despite being shot numerous times, but for Veronika Weiss and Katherine Cooper, it was too late. They both died on the sidewalk. All three were members of the Delta Delta Delta sorority.

Veronika Weiss was known as a tomboy who played four sports in high school while also earning straight A's. Both her mother and grandmother also belong to Delta Delta Delta. Her friends thought of her as being mature beyond her years. Cooper was an art history and archaeology student at UC Santa Barbara. She was known as being outgoing and helpful to all.

Elliot didn't consider Delta Delta Delta the hottest sorority around. Somewhere amidst all of his adrenaline and panic, he must have been a tad disappointed. This had already gone a bit sideways. He wasn't able to kidnap and torture anyone, nor was he able to get into his chosen sorority and murder beautiful women one by one. He already was reduced to shooting at random people on the street and trying to hit them with his car.

He drove a few blocks and shot indiscriminately into a coffee shop, which was closed and then continued down the street.

Christopher Michaels-Martinez, the only child of two San Luis Obispo attorneys, was standing in front of a nearby Deli Mart when he heard gunfire. He and several other frightened people attempted to get inside the deli when a bullet struck and killed him. Known as being an avid reader and impressive athlete, he had planned to spend a year studying in London.

Elliot continued to fire numerous gunshots into the store, then drove away firing randomly at people on the sidewalk. He continued speeding down the wrong side of the street, striking a pedestrian who was attempting to cross the road.

The madness continued. Bailey Maples had just left a restaurant called Pizza My Heart with her friend Aaron Zaglin, when she saw a black BMW come to a stop next to them. Elliot rolled down the window, said something she couldn't understand, then laughed in a way she later described as "creepy." Then he took out a gun, pointed at her, and started shooting. He hit her in the arm, and she ran back inside the restaurant. She heard a few more shots and heard the windows of the store shatter.

Elliot continued on his way, shooting randomly, hitting a female bicyclist with a bullet in the thigh. She later described him as smiling when he shot her.

Elliot turned east on Del Playa Drive, then did a U-turn and went west where he encountered county sheriff Adrien Marquez. Marquez was on foot when he saw the BMW driving by. He took a shot at it, and Elliot fired back. Both shots did no damage.

Hannah Miller and Sierra Swartz were walking in the area when they heard something that sounded like gunshots, but they weren't sure, as fireworks were a common event in Isla Vista. It was a party town after all. Out of nowhere, a black BMW came up to them at a high rate of speed and stopped in the middle of the road. Swartz later described the driver as a "totally normal" guy with brown hair, wearing sunglasses.

Swartz said "What's up? to him and kept walking. This is when Elliot pulled up a gun and held it in his right hand close to his chest, not pointing it out the window. She then heard a shot. She was surprised she wasn't hit since she was so close to Elliot and wondered if the gun was even real. He had a weird little grin on his face.

While his Day of Retribution certainly wasn't as awe inspiring as he hoped, he was causing an incredible amount of mayhem. Still, it couldn't have been enough for Elliot. It wasn't like he was being treated as a God or anything. Quite the contrary, he only had a few minutes left before he was dead.

Elliot continued along, shooting randomly out the window, sideswiping parked vehicles and hitting bicyclists with his car. Although it seemed to those in the area that this had been going on for hours, in reality the whole thing lasted a matter of minutes.

Finally, he encountered four officers who were on foot near Little Acorn Park, at the corner of Sabado Tarde Road and El Embarcadero Road. Elliot shot at them and missed. The officers returned fire, shooting numerous rounds at him as he drove away at high speed. One of the shots struck Elliot in the hip. One has to wonder how that felt to Elliot, thinking of himself as such a such a gentleman and all, to feel the sting of a bullet.

One of the officers was later quoted as saying: "Not only did I feel like my life was threatened, I felt like every person in Isla Vista was threatened. This guy was just driving around like a crazy person shooting at whoever he could shoot at. I felt it was my duty to take that shot if I had the shot."

All of a sudden police were everywhere pursuing Elliot, who was wounded, bleeding, and almost certainly quite depressed. While it is obviously reprehensible to kill 6 people and wound 14 others, which was Elliot's final toll, this wasn't quite the Day of Retribution Elliot had in mind. He hadn't accomplished any of his goals. It was more like a Day of Lunacy.

His final act against the world was to graze a bicyclist with his BMW before crashing into a row of parked cars at 9:35 p.m. Other than ambushing and murdering his roommates in a rather cowardly way, his "Day of Retribution" had lasted all of eight minutes.

Elliot was found in the BMW dead, with a single, self-inflicted gunshot wound to the head. Elliot had killed himself.

When officers arrived at the scene of the accident, they saw the BMW engulfed in smoke, the driver's side door open, and the suspect lying next to the door. There was blood everywhere. Elliot had an entry wound on one side of his head and an exit wound on the other; brain matter was visible.

In the car were three, 9-millimeter, semi-automatic pistols. Only one of the pistols, a Sig Sauer, had been fired. Deputies pulled his dead body out of the car and handcuffed his corpse.

In the early morning hours of May 25, detectives entered Elliot's apartment where they found the bodies of his roommates.

Elliot's room was quite the mess. His laptop was open to YouTube, where they saw he had uploaded his "retribution" video, the one where he let the world know of his plans for the day. The video eventually went viral before it was pulled from YouTube, but one can still find it, if one spends a bit of time looking around.

Elliot's sheets and pillows were slashed and stabbed, leaving detectives to surmise that he was practicing before he attacked his roomies, or maybe he was just psyching himself up. They found a shirt and jeans caked in blood on the bed.

Also in his room, they found numerous lottery tickets, the book *Art of Seduction,* games such as *Call of Duty, World of Warcraft,* and *Halo,* as well as Monster Energy drinks and a Starbucks coffee cup. They also found knives, a hammer, and empty boxes of ammunition, as well as a printed copy of his manifesto *My Twisted World.*

There was a journal Elliot had written by hand. The last page said: "I had to tear some pages out because I feared my intentions would be discovered. I taped them back together as fast as I could. This is it. In one hour I will have my revenge on this cruel world. I HATE YOU ALLLL! DIE."

His iPhone had 492 images and videos on it, of which 200 were selfies. One video of Elliot complained about how lazy his roomies were, while another showed him in tears because two women, who he said hello to on the street, ignored him.

His Internet history was random, scattered, and disturbing with such searches as "Did Adolf Hitler have a girlfriend" and "Nazi anime." Others included "quick silent kill with a knife," "how to kill someone with a knife," "Xingjian railway station terrorist knife attack explosion bombing," "roommate takes very long showers," and "modern torture devices." He also searched for porn.

One of his last online posts was on puahate.com: He wrote: "You're all jealous of my 10/10 pretty-boy face. This site is full of stupid, disgusting, mentally ill degenerates who take pleasure in putting down others. That is all I have to say on here. Goodbye."

THINGS GO AWRY

Elliot Oliver Robertson Rodger was born to his father Peter Rodger, and his mother Chin, in a London, England, hospital on July 24, 1991. Elliot was small at birth. He weighed just 5.4 pounds.

Elliot came from an impressive family, one that had its share of prestige and success. Peter Rodger was a tall, handsome, and confident man as well as an award-winning photographer and director. At the time of Elliot's birth, Peter was known for his work in high-profile advertising campaigns. Later in life, he had the position of second director in the film *The Hunger Games* and produced and funded his own documentary titled *Oh My God?*

The Rodger family was well placed in British circles and was once known as being very wealthy although the family fortune had taken a bit of a hit during the Great Depression. Peter's father, George, was a photojournalist who rose to the top of his field in large part because of his work depicting concentration camp deaths in WWII. His photos documenting piles of corpses at the Bergen-Belsen concentration camp were featured in *Time Magazine* as well as *Life*. George Rodger gave up working as a war correspondent when he came to the realization that he spent much of his time looking at piles of corpses trying to figure out what would be the most stylish and artistically pleasing photo of them.

Elliot's mother, Chin, born in Malaysia, was a very attractive woman. She knew many people in the film industry, including George Lucas, who she dated for a while before she met Peter. She was rumored to have also dated Steven Spielberg. Although Peter and Chin had been together for a few years, the pregnancy was not planned.

When Elliot was born, his family lived in London, but, as they had just started a family, they soon moved to a large house in the country. Peter was on his way up in the photography business and was making enough money for Chin to quit her job as a nurse to stay home and raise Elliot. Elliot's maternal grandmother also lived with the family and helped with his care at times.

When it came time, Elliot went to an expensive all boys' preschool called Dorsett House. Right from the start he was nervous when he had to be around other children. He wasn't happy at all his life had to change. He cried uncontrollably on his first day of school. He didn't like all the rules and didn't understand why he had to follow them. He hated the uniform in large part because he had to wear socks up to his knees, which he thought made him look ridiculous, and he had to play soccer.

It wasn't that he hated the game; it was that he found that he wasn't able to compete with the other boys. They were stronger and faster than he was. He stood near the goalie, pretending that he was being helpful, hoping no one would notice how awful he was. He called himself the "goalie's assistant."

There were happy times too. Elliot often spent time at a range of hills near his house with his father flying kites. He called them the "London Hills" because in his imagination the vibrant city of London was right on the other side of whatever hill he happened to be on. Early on his father did all of the work flying the kites with Elliot watching, or at times they might attempt to do it together, but soon he learned to fly them all on his own. While he felt proud of this, he was always afraid the wind would pick up his tiny body along with the kite and carry him away.

The family traveled often and by the age of four, Elliot had been to France, Spain, Greece, Malaysia, and the United States. Even at a young age Elliot knew that he was living a special and privileged life.

It was on a trip to Greece that his family heard the news of the death of Peter's father, George, at the age of 87. They immediately flew home. It was the first time Elliot saw his father cry.

While Peter was successful as a photographer, he had higher ambitions. His true desire was to become a film director and knew that if he really wanted to succeed on a grand stage, he would need to move to the United States. Around the same time that Peter was entertaining this notion, Chin became pregnant again. Elliot soon had a sister named Georgia.

Elliot was now five. The thought of moving to America terrified him, but he was excited at the same time, especially when he found out his new house might have a swimming pool. How special would that be? After much hand wringing and decision making, the Rodger family made the move across the pond.

When the family arrived in America, they settled in a large house in the town of Woodland Hills, an upscale area bordering the Santa Monica mountains. It's known as a place one could take a hike through a beautiful canyon in the morning, do some upscale shopping in the afternoon, and go out to a lovely dinner at night. It was also close enough to the action for Peter to be active in the entertainment business. It was a large home with white walls, and indeed did have a gated swimming pool, so it met young Elliot's specifications.

Up until then, until the grand old age of five, Elliot still considered himself "happy." He was wealthy, at least to his young mind, and he was now an American. He was looking forward to all life had to offer. His father agreed that these were good times. He was later quoted as saying that those years were "wonderous" and that Elliot was a "really adorable cute little boy."

He was enrolled in a private school for kindergarten. His first real friend in the United States was a girl named Maddy, who Elliot described as "the first female friend I've ever had, and she would be the last."

Although Elliot enjoyed life at this time, there was a reason for that. He had yet to care about the female sex and cared even less what they thought of him. As he wrote, he also was "completely oblivious of the fact that my future on this world would only turn to darkness and misery because of girls."

Elliot used to take baths with Maddy when he was young. Elliot didn't think anything of this normal activity at the time, but as the years passed, he would recall how this was the only time in real life he would see a girl of any age naked. In his mind he had peaked at age five.

Later in his life he would miss these innocent days. He thought of them as being a time when everyone started out together and were on the same team, where people tried to help each other out. This was all before he began to think the majority of people were his enemies. Before his hatred started. Before he thought people were awful.

He enjoyed kindergarten and everything it had to offer; he had playdates, and he hung out with a lot of different kids. All was going well. Soon he turned six. He had a wonderful Disney-themed birthday party and invited all his friends, except for one who Elliot felt had been mean to him. He took great joy in leaving him out.

Elliot and his father used to go to a park together, mostly to spend time at the playground. He remembered this time fondly except for one thing. When he played on the swings, his father had to push him for him to reach any sort of height, while other boys could swing by themselves, even ones that were younger than he was. This would make little Elliot jealous. He couldn't understand why this was so hard for him to swing and go way up high in the air and so easy for others. It reminded him of when he used to play soccer and realized he wasn't on par physically with the other kids.

The thing was, much to his horror, Elliot was still small. One day his family went to Universal Studios. He was very much into dinosaurs then and had just seen Jurassic Park, so of course he was dying to go on the Jurassic Park ride. It was what he was looking forward to most of all.

He waited for an hour in line with his family, the excitement building to a crescendo. He could barely contain himself, and often asked his father how much longer it would be before it was his time. When he finally got to the front of the line, he put his head up against the measuring stick and was told by a very unenthusiastic employee that he was too short to go on the ride. He fell apart. As he sat there crying in utmost shame, other boys that appeared to be his age walked past and got on the ride that he coveted so much. For the first time, he was denied something he wanted because of his size. But in his mind it wouldn't be the last. As he wrote: "Little did I know, this injustice was very small indeed compared to all the things I'll be denied in the future because of my height."

Elliot attended Topanga Elementary School when it came time for first grade. He was nervous about not knowing any of the other kids, but despite his apprehension, all went well and Elliot was treated kindly. The family moved once again into a new house, which had a fabulous view of the Santa Monica Mountains, and of course another swimming pool.

Peter Rodger's career was going well. He was starting to direct commercials that had large budgets. This was good for his career and his bank account, but meant he was away from home a lot, leaving Elliot with his mother and often a nanny to care for him. While he missed his father, he was impressed by how important he seemed to be.

Elliot made his first true friend at this point, a boy named James. The two lived nearby and the hung out all the time. For Christmas that year Elliot got a Nintendo 64. Elliot loved this game; it was a whole new world for him. He and his father bonded while spending a lot of time playing it together.

Elliot started to notice that Peter and Chin began to argue often. He wasn't too concerned at the thought of them splitting up; it never even occurred to him that such a thing could happen. But he did find it unpleasant. No child likes to see their parents fight, and Elliot was more sensitive than most.

The fights continued. One day Elliot asked his mother if she and Peter might ever stop being together. She told him no, of course not. But a few months later that was exactly what happened. Soon after Elliot turned seven, his parents divorced. Elliot, who was prone to histrionics even when things were going okay, didn't take it well.

His mother moved to another house, and Elliot and his sister spent most of their time with her, then stayed with his father on the weekends. Peter paid child support.

Elliot would later write that after this, his life changed forever. Of course a lot of children go through divorce and don't wind up killing all sorts of people, so perhaps this should be taken with a grain of salt.

His mother moved to a house in Topanga. It was just a two-bedroom house, so Elliot had to share a room with his sister, which in his mind was quite beneath his lot in life. He wasn't happy about any of this, but, as always, his mother was kind to Elliot and made him feel as comfortable as she could.

On the weekends, Elliot returned to his father's house, but he was often sad without his mother's presence. He wrote that she was the one thing that made him feel safe and secure, and it was worse for him to be at a place where his family was once all together, there were too many sad memories.

Second grade soon started and most of the kids in his class were the same as in first grade, but Elliot's friend James was gone. He had moved to another town, although they continued to stay in touch as they would for years.

It seemed that Peter couldn't quite afford such a large house as the one the family was living in, what with the financial implications of the divorce. He moved to a smaller house also in Topanga Canyon, an artsy bohemian town filled with stunning views. The house was in a rural area with hiking trails that lead to nearby mountains. Although Elliot was saddened by the changes in his life, he spent much time outside exploring and going on adventures. Nature was always something that could sooth Elliot, as least a little bit.

One day, just a few months after his seventh birthday, Elliot went to his father's house after school only to see a woman standing in the kitchen who introduced herself to him as Soumaya. She was a beautiful woman with a very exotic look.

Peter told Elliot that she was going to be living with them from now on. Elliot assumed she was just a friend who would be staying with them, or perhaps a nanny of some sort, as it seemed unimaginable to him that his father could already be with someone new, romantically. It also seemed odd to him a woman that he had never even met was to live with him. But he soon figured out that Soumaya was in fact his de facto stepmother. This totally confused Elliot. How could this be?

As bewildered as little Elliot was by this new situation, it also made him respect his father more than ever. To Elliot it was obvious Peter was a man women wanted. He was powerful and desirable. To have split up with his mother and almost immediately found some other woman who would want to be with him, showed Elliot that Peter was a true leader in the world, an alpha who took what he wanted.

Soumaya was an aspiring actress who had appeared in some small roles in television and film, most notably *Les Vraies Housewives*, the French adaptation of "Real Housewives." She was from Morocco and the product of a wealthy family. Elliot soon became used to her presence around the house. It wasn't as awkward as he first thought it would be. He even liked her at first. He thought she was fun; she and Elliot often played and joked around. It was nice for him to have someone else to spend time with.

But soon she began to discipline Elliot and did so in a harsher way than he was accustomed to. Since she wasn't even his real parent, this bothered him quite a bit. He felt she didn't have any right to tell him what to do, and even less of a right to punish him. Also, nannies began to take care of Elliot when he was at his father's house, some stayed only briefly, others for years.

Life went on. Elliot still spent time with his friend James even though they didn't live as close to each other anymore. With Elliot being shy, it was hard for him to make new friends. Because of James's influence, Elliot started getting into Pokémon, both on his Gameboy and by collecting cards. Not everything was mundane though. He attended the premiere of *Star Wars Episode 1* because of his mother's continued friendship with George Lucas. This was quite exciting for him. He felt special.

Despite his upheaval at home, elementary school was going well, although he could make no sense of girls. As Elliot wrote:

> *It was as if the girls in elementary school were part of a separate reality. Despite not having much interaction with them, they treated me cordially, as they treated all other boys of my age. This was fair, and I was content with this. I hadn't gone through puberty yet, and so I had no desire for female validation. My eight-year-old self had no inkling*

of the pain and misery girls would cause me once puberty would inevitably arrive and my sexual desires for girls would develop. Sexual desires that would be mercilessly spurned. Some of the boys in my class would grow up to be embraced by girls, while I would grow up to be rejected by them. But at that moment in time, we were just innocent children growing up together. All innocence is destined to be shattered and replaced with bitter brutality. I was living in ignorant, innocent bliss. And I was happy with it.

Around the holidays, Elliot and his family spent some time in Morocco visiting Soumaya's family, and also made a stop in England on the way home. Elliot continued to lead a privileged life, whether he realized it or not.

His father was becoming more successful in his career in film and with that came signs of opulence. The family moved into a five-bedroom house with a pool near Woodland Hills, which is quite the desirable neighborhood. Despite his father's apparent wealth, and Elliot's desire for such trappings, he still preferred to spend time with his mother, as he found her kind and fun, much more so than his father and Soumaya.

It was around this time that his parents started to become concerned with Elliot's mental health. There are conflicting reports as to whether Elliot was ever diagnosed with Asperger's syndrome, which is a form of autism, as a child. His mother believed he had these issues and was quoted in a sworn statement in divorce documents in which she asked for more child support: "Elliot has special needs. He is a high functioning autistic child." Although some might point to this diagnosis as a factor in Elliot's later actions, there is no concrete evidence or reliable studies showing any significant difference in violent behavior when it comes to people on the autism spectrum.

Peter didn't agree with that diagnosis and claimed in the same court document that he was not aware of any diagnosis of Asperger's syndrome, although he did think there was something going on with him. During an interview with Barbara Walters on *ABC News*, Peter said Elliot had "a certain OCD" about him, always putting his plate in the same place at the dinner table, always wearing the same clothes."

Throughout his short life, Elliot was never hospitalized for mental illness, although he received sporadic treatment up until his death. There is no doubt Elliot was severely depressed as an adult, and he suffered from acute social phobia. While at points in his life, he did mention to mental health professionals that he had considered suicide, he never showed any aggression towards others.

When he was a child, he often would cry when he was in a large crowd and would rather write information down as opposed to speaking. When he did speak, he spoke in almost a whisper. He would at times make repetitive noises or tap his feet incessantly. In class, teachers said he was often unresponsive. He didn't participate unless forced to and often would just stare off into space or at an object. If loud noises occurred, he would put his hands over his ears and often repeated the words "great" and "cool." Many thought he displayed behaviors similar to Asperger's syndrome.

During recess, he would often hide behind buildings waiting for the bell to ring before he would emerge again, so he could head to the relative safety of class. He was a perfectionist and showed many signs of being obsessive compulsive. He needed to have everything on his desk in a perfect order or he would become very upset.

He was a very picky eater. He would have nothing with any sort of sauce on it, and anything that was "gooey" at all, such as melted cheese, was just totally out of the question. He had a hard time going to birthday parties, as he wouldn't eat any of the food and hated to participate in any sort of activities with the other kids.

Elliot wasn't worried about this kind of thing all that much though. He was way more worried about his height. Elliot continued to be short for his age. At the start of fourth grade, he realized to his horror he was the smallest boy in his class. This was humiliating to him, and he made a plan that would rectify the situation. He began to play basketball, as he convinced himself, that if he did so, it would make him taller, as opposed to recognizing tall people tend to play basketball. He would play for hours on public courts, or by himself on the court at his father's house. Sometimes when he was by himself and no one else could see, he would lay on the ground and stretch, willing himself to grow.

That wasn't the only problem though. He noticed that other boys could throw a ball twice as far as he could. To his great dismay, Elliot soon began to realize he was not only short, but weak as well.

Elliot continued to hang out with his friend James, but it always went much better when it was just the two of them with no other friends around. When James would have other friends over for playdates as well, Elliot would often become jealous and cry in a corner.

But things weren't that bad, at least compared to how they would become for Elliot. He was just getting warmed up. As he wrote:

> *Jealousy and envy... those are two feelings that would dominate my entire life and bring me immense pain. The feelings of jealousy I felt at nine-years-old were frustrating, but they were nothing compared to how I would feel once I hit puberty and have to watch girls choosing other boys over me. Any problem I had at nine-years-old was nirvana compared to what I was doomed to face.*

HOW TO BE COOL

While Elliot was spending time at his father's house, two South American nannies looked after him. They spoke little English, but they were kind to him, and to Elliot that was all that really mattered. But, even with the extra help with his care, he started having more difficulties with Soumaya. She wasn't used to having children around, especially one as particular as Elliot, and he wasn't used to being told what to do.

Since she wasn't his actual parent, Elliot hated the rules she made him follow and felt that she was way too strict with him. Who did she even think she was to tell him what to do? Every night she insisted on making him eat a type of soup that he hated. He made such a big deal about how much he disliked it that she started making him eat the soup as a punishment.

By contrast, his mother arranged playdates for Elliot as he was too shy to do it himself, and treated him with unending kindness. He loved her so back then. He started to hate going home to his father's, especially as Peter was rarely there because he was so busy with work. When his mother dropped him off at his father's house, he often cried when his mother drove away. This just made the rift between Elliot and Soumaya worse.

Elliot was only nine years old, but he already had begun to think about life's inequities. He spent much of his time ruminating about how some people were higher up in society than others; they just seemed better somehow. People liked them right away, life was so easy for them. He wanted to be one of those people; even at a young age it was the most important thing in the world for him. He had no idea how to do it, but he certainly was going to try.

At school there were the cool kids; the ones that knew how to act and how to dress and were adored for it, and then there were the rest of the herd—those who simply didn't matter. He didn't want to be one of those people, the ones that were ignored and forgotten. He wanted to be at the top of the heap. To Elliot things had already begun to change. There were to be no more times where everyone was on the same level. The competition had begun. He wanted to win.

As Elliot wrote:

> *When I became aware of this common social structure at my school, I also started to examine myself and compare myself to these "cool kids." I realized, with some horror, that I wasn't "cool" at all. I had a dorky hairstyle, I wore plain and uncool clothing, and I was shy and unpopular. I was always described as the shy boy in the past, but I never really thought my shyness would affect me in a negative way, until this point. I envied the cool kids, and I wanted to be one of them. I was a bit frustrated at my parents for not shaping me into one of these kids in the past. They never made an effort to dress me in stylish clothing or get me a good-looking haircut. I had to make every effort to rectify this. I had to adapt.*

The first thing Elliot did on his new mission to be cool was bleach his hair blonde. He had thought of doing it for quite a while and finally worked up his nerve. When he had blonde hair, he would get attention, and it would show the world how cool he was. It was obvious to him his old hair was part of what was holding him back.

He was so nervous when he went to school sporting his new look. What if no one noticed, or, even worse, thought he looked stupid? What if he was made fun of? Elliot was always anxious at school, but this day was even worse. Thankfully a few kids told him that his hair looked awesome. Others seemed to think the same, kids seemed to look at him and notice him for once.

For a while he convinced himself he actually *was* cool, and that helped for a bit. But he had to do more, blonde hair was simply not enough. He stopped playing Pokémon, as he heard from others it wasn't a thing that the in-crowd did anymore.

It seemed that most of the popular kids skateboarded, so Elliot resolved to do so as well. How hard could it be? Between his totally cool hair and becoming an excellent skateboarder he hoped he would be the coolest kid ever.

He got his father to buy him a nice board and soon started practicing regularly, sometimes for hours a day. He didn't let anyone see him skate at first though, for when he first showed everyone he could skateboard, he wanted to be excellent. To Elliot, there was no point in skateboarding if he couldn't impress people. He wanted to have people see him skateboard and look at him in awe.

Fourth grade ended and he decided, that over the summer, he was going to make himself the coolest kid one could imagine, so he could be popular when he went back to school. He couldn't wait to be so awesome, to be popular.

His father moved again, to an even bigger house in an exclusive area of Woodland Hills. Elliot had a bedroom with his own private bathroom and a balcony.

He continued to work on skateboarding and got his friend James into it, so he had someone to practice with. It was hard to stay motivated doing it by himself all the time. They spent much of the summer working on their skills and going to skateparks. Elliot began to buy a lot of skate clothes, so he would look the part. He felt this whole cool thing was working.

Soon the fall came, and it was time for him to see all his hard work come to fruition. Elliot had high hopes for success with his new vibe. As he wrote :

> *For the first week of Fifth Grade, I was at mother's house. I considered myself to be very "cool" by now. I had gotten better at skateboarding, I had blonde hair, and I dressed like a skateboarder. I felt great anticipation for what the cool kids would think of me once they saw my transformation. To my disappointment, no one really cared. They were all in their own worlds. I don't remember any kids showing recognition of my new "coolness."*

He did make a few inroads and started hanging with some kids he considered to be the popular crowd a bit more. But, for the most part, all his work had been a waste of time. This was incredibly disappointing to Elliot. He felt he had wasted much of his summer.

He still hated being at his father's, as Peter and Soumaya didn't pay a ton of attention to him, in his opinion at least. He wanted to feel special, and that just wasn't happening there. Also, most of his "cool" clothes were at his mother's, and he hated having to dress like a nerd in the clothing at his father's house. His mother had moved closer to his father, so at least Elliot could walk back and forth between homes.

Elliot didn't give up on his dreams of coolness. He kept working at becoming better at skateboarding, maybe the issue was he simply wasn't good enough to impress everyone. His mother took him to the park regularly to practice tricks. He wanted to be a pro skateboarder, that was his dream. He pictured himself skating in front of a group of screaming and adoring fans. Still, he and the cool kids never really became friends. Even if a popular kid paid any sort of attention to Elliot, he looked at them more as competition than people to hang out with.

Soumaya continued to overstep her boundaries, in Elliot's mind. He simply couldn't figure out why she kept trying to tell him what to do. Didn't she have anything else to do except sit around and ruin Elliot's life?

She forced Elliot to try and become friends with some of the neighborhood kids, as she was afraid he had no social life. This was true, but Elliot didn't want anyone to acknowledge it, much less try to do something about it.

Soumaya began to make him leave the house and refused to let him back in until he introduced himself to the other kids. Elliot was terrified. These kids were skateboarders too, and even worse, they were the "cool" type. Elliot often went outside as she suggested, and when he came home he pretended to Soumaya he was playing with them, but in reality he just hid in the woods or behind the house, hoping to convince Soumaya on his return he had made friends. But she somehow always knew the truth. Finally much to his dismay, Soumaya had the nanny bring Elliot to where the kids were hanging out and had her ask if Eliot could play with them. Elliot was shocked when these kids were actually nice to him and let him skateboard with them for the day. He never really hung out with them again, but at least it got Soumaya off his back.

When it came to school, things weren't going as well as Elliot wanted. He wasn't as popular as he should be, at least in his opinion, and he had no real group of friends that he could call his own. Still, he regarded his status as more successful than prior years. He didn't want it to end. Not because he loved school so much but because of what was looming in his future. As much as elementary school wasn't a walk in the park, middle school was next, and Elliot was terrified.

He was mostly terrified about interacting with girls. He knew from watching TV and movies that this was the time when girls would become something he would be expected to have success with if he were to be "cool" in any way. Soon he might be expected to kiss a girl, or even have a girlfriend, and this filled him with dread. How was he ever going to get the respect and admiration he deserved if he wasn't able to have a girlfriend in middle school?

He wrote:

> *As children we all play together as equals in a fair environment. Only after the advent of puberty does the true brutality of human nature show its face. Life will become a bitter and unfair struggle for self-worth, all because girls will choose some boys over others. The boys who girls find attractive will live pleasure-filled lives while they dominate the boys who girls deem unworthy. Matt Bordier (a popular kid at school) will go on to live a life of pleasure. Girls will throw themselves at him. And I will go on to be rejected and humiliated by girls. At that moment in time, we were just playing together as children, oblivious to the fact that my future will be dark and his will be bright. Life is such a cruel joke.*

Although he had practiced very hard, Elliot wasn't good enough at skateboarding to be as impressive as he hoped. To his great dismay, he noticed some boys that were younger than he was could do more tricks than he could. To Elliot it was just another failure, another thing that he sucked at. He could never get something as simple as a kickflip down. All he could do was ollie a bit and go down some mediocre ramps without falling over. Then at the park he would see some random eight-year-old kickflip like it was nothing. This was beyond humiliating to Elliot and made him so angry. He felt like a failure at everything. So he stopped. He hated skateboarding now.

He was terrified all summer of going to middle school. At moments he would relax and feel safe and was able to calm himself down, but then he would remember what his future held in just a few short months, and he felt afraid all over again. He wasn't ready. Life would never be the same.

When the first day came, he literally shook with fear. His mind was roiling with anxiety. He was going to a new school where he knew no one. He tried to act confident, but it was no use. He was certain they could all see right through him.

When school started, he noticed right away there were two groups of cool kids: the skateboarder types and the ones that were comfortable with girls. Elliot wasn't either of them. Although in reality he was pretty good, in his mind Elliot sucked at skateboarding and was about as uncomfortable with girls as he could possibly imagine. He felt intimidated by the cool kids, and in turn hated them for making him feel that way. He thought they were all a bunch of jerks.

Worse yet, most of the girls were taller than he was. He had always been short, but now it seemed so pronounced. He felt ridiculous. There was a particular group of girls Elliot found very pretty. He thought about them all the time, but none of them ever noticed him. All of them hung around with one particular boy named Robert. This made Elliot seethe with anger. What did Robert have that he didn't? Why was he so special?

He was disgusted by the cool kids, but he still wanted to be them. Well, he wanted to be them except different. He didn't want to be what he considered to be a stupid savage. He thought they were idiots, that they were jerks, and yet they were also the boys that the girls seemed to like the best. To Elliot, this proved once more what an awful place the world was. He began to think humans were nothing but dumb animals.

As Elliot wrote:

Everything my father taught me was proven wrong. He raised me to be a polite, kind gentleman. In a decent world, that would be ideal. But the polite, kind gentleman doesn't win in the real world. The girls don't flock to the gentlemen. They flock to the alpha male. They flock to the boys who appear to have the most power and status. And it was a ruthless struggle to reach such a height.

It seemed to Elliot that the one true way to be "cool" was girls had to like him. But how could he accomplish this? Elliot thought girls were complete fools, drawn to the type of man that Elliot could never be, the type that he didn't even want to be. Sure, he could do something wild with his hair, buy a stylish shirt, maybe even keep trying to skateboard; but he had no idea how to make girls like him. Elliot retreated into himself even more, becoming even more shy and withdrawn.

A few kids were nice to him, some of them were even part of the popular crowd. As much as he hated them, whenever one of them was nice to him, he became happy and sated, like the world was okay for a bit. Like he mattered, like he was seen. Some of the girls at the school were kind to him. He got an occasional hug from one of them, which made him feel amazing, accepted, and whole. But still none of them actually seemed to be interested in him as a potential boyfriend. He felt he was treated as a harmless pet.

He even worked up enough confidence to go to a school dance. Some of the older girls that were in seventh and eighth grades offered to dance with him, being kind to a kid who was so obviously shy. They danced with him, Elliot's hands on their hips, with their hands on his shoulders as they were taller, of course. They danced slowly; their bodies almost touching. Elliot was in Heaven. He would later say this was the only time of his life when he ever had a good experience with girls.

While outwardly, his father was doing well, in reality he was struggling financially. He reduced the child support he was paying to Chin. Elliot and his mother had to move to a smaller house in a middle-class area. Elliot found it demeaning to live there. It wasn't nearly a nice enough house for him to live in, but he still preferred it over staying at his father's home. His mother was still kind to him and her home was his safe place. In his words, she made "everything better." But Elliot was upset she wasn't rich.

Try as he might to become more popular, it wasn't really taking. Although there was the occasional girl that gave Elliot a hug, and many that would say hello, it was obvious to him that he wasn't truly cool. He was barely accepted. This ate away at him daily.

He began hanging out from time to time with a boy named Connor. He was a popular boy who bullied Elliot and pushed him around in front of others, but it was okay, at least he had someone to spend time with, to keep the wolves at bay. He was hanging out with Connor after all. That at least hinted at coolness.

Once, Connor came over to the home where Elliot lived with his mother to hang out. It went all right, at least Elliot thought so until Connor went back to school and told everyone that Elliot was poor. This bothered Elliot to an incredible degree. He spent much time doing damage control, telling others at school how wealthy his father was, even going as far as to bring in photos of his father's house to show everyone how good he really had it. While this may have had the desired effect in the short term, in the long term it did much more damage than if Elliot had just left Connor's claims alone. No one likes someone desperate, and Elliot had desperation seeping through his every pore.

Right around this time, Elliot met his true best friend. The Internet. It was still somewhat new, and Elliot couldn't believe all the opportunities it brought to him. Elliot started an AOL instant messenger account and began to explore the net. His mother gave him an hour a day to be on the computer, which he used to join chat rooms and talk to strangers all over the world. He was amazed and intrigued that he could talk to so many people from all sorts of different backgrounds. He still didn't have any real friends he could rely on, but he soon met some online, people that got him, that he could be himself with. Kind of anyway, as much as anyone could online. This filled a hole inside of him. Or at least it came close.

Once, someone that Elliot met through a chatroom mailed him some photos of naked women. Elliot was shocked, afraid and more, than a little bit creeped out. He didn't like the way the women looked in the photos and, even more, he didn't like the way he felt. Was that what women really looked like down there? He didn't message that person back again.

Elliot was going to be in seventh grade soon. He knew things were going to change for him, and he had no idea how to handle it. Sixth grade was bad enough, now he had to deal with seventh? And he worried it would just get worse from there. When would the changes end? He still wanted to be a child. He didn't want to worry about being popular, about girls liking him, but yet he did worry about such things. Constantly. All day he would ruminate about how to become popular, and all night when he tried to go to sleep, he perseverated. Was there something wrong with him? He thought this impossible. There must be something wrong with everyone else.

He was too shy to even talk to girls; they made him feel nervous, inferior. He wanted them so badly, but he had no idea what to say to them. He hated the popular boys, but despite his hate, he still wanted desperately for them to like him. He wanted friends. He wanted girls to like him. He wanted to be someone. But none of this was happening, in fact things seem to be getting worse.

During summer he spent much of his time inside playing *Halo* on the new Xbox his mother had given him. He didn't see his friend James much anymore although he was still his best friend. He had no interest in doing anything and didn't go anywhere unless he was forced to. He wanted to be left alone. His mother noticed all of this and much to Elliot's dismay sent him to summer camp.

He hated it. He felt nervous. Awkward. One day while at camp, Elliot was playing with some other kids when they started to tickle him. This happened a lot because of how susceptible to ticking he was. It's one of those things; once kids find out someone is ticklish, it's all over.

He accidentally bumped into a girl, who just happened to be very pretty, when trying to get away from his tormentors. She swore at Elliot and pushed him. She called him stupid. He was mortified. Later he wrote that the incident "scarred him for life," saying:

> *I couldn't believe what had happened. Cruel treatment from women is ten times worse than from men. It made me feel like an insignificant, unworthy little mouse. I felt so small and vulnerable. I couldn't believe that this girl was so horrible to me, and I thought that it was because she viewed me as a loser. That was the first experience of female cruelty I endured, and it traumatized me to no end. It made me even more nervous around girls, and I would be extremely weary (sic) and cautious of them from that point on. I felt relieved when summer camp ended. That experience with the mean girl ruined it for me. Hell, it ruined a part of my life. Whenever I think about summer camp I would think about that girl, and my emotions would flare up.*

THE PROBLEM WITH GIRLS

The summer wasn't all bad. Elliot knew a boy named John Jo who introduced him to a cyber cafe called Planet Cyber. In those days not everyone had a laptop, or even a computer at home, so there were places where people went to use public computers, to play games, and even do things like check their email or do some work.

Elliot began to go to the cafe often and play online games with others. It was within walking distance of his house and was something for him to do. Soon, Elliot was in love. It was a romance that would last most of his short life. He found someplace where he could escape from the world, and escape he did.

Those first beautiful days, he played *Day of Defeat* and *Counter Strike*, but soon he would start playing an RPG, called *Diablo 2*. An RPG is a Role Playing Game that allows players to have their own character in a fictional setting, which was not only fun for Elliot, it also gave him the ability to interact with other players online as well. While RPG's are now commonplace, back then they were mind blowing.

John Jo and another friend named Charlie began to sleep over at Elliot's house on occasion, and the three often went to hang out at Planet Cyber. Elliot later described these times as some of the best experiences of his life. He had friends that liked what he liked, and all were on an equal footing. He had a bit of a tribe.

Soon though seventh grade started, and all the anxiety came flooding back. He still had none of the social acceptance he craved so desperately, and he had to witness others who he deemed unworthy enjoy themselves unencumbered. Elliot became angry that some kids, even though they might be what he called "chubby-faced" or "obnoxious louts" and "imbeciles" were popular, while Elliott was not. He was even more upset that an "obnoxious Mexican kid" who was new to the school immediately became popular purely because he was cocky.

This is the type of thinking that cursed Elliot throughout his life. He wanted people to not judge him, but he constantly judged others. He didn't just want friends; he wanted his friends to be popular. He didn't just want a girlfriend; he wanted a beautiful girlfriend. There is no doubt there were certainly many short girls and women who were not amazingly attractive who noticed Elliot, but of course he didn't want them; they were beneath him. He probably never even noticed them.

Elliot was not totally unpopular at this point, he didn't have any friends from school that he spent time with, but he wasn't picked on either. He was just the shy kid no one seemed to pay attention to.

He still hung out on the weekend with John Jo, Charlie, and another friend named Elijah. Sometimes they slept over at Elliot's house, but they almost always hung out together and went to Planet Cyber, where they played games for hours on end. Sometimes they stayed there until three in the morning. Elliot later described this as the only social group he ever really was involved with.

This was the extent of Elliot's social life. Most other things were too painful for him to do. For example, he didn't like going to the movies because it just reminded him of what his life lacked. He felt humiliated and jealous seeing couples hanging out, or groups of friends going to see a film. That was one thing about Planet Cyber, there certainly weren't any couples going there to hang out together.

He still hadn't begun puberty, which in Elliot's mind was a good thing. He dreaded it. As he wrote: "I barely even knew much about what puberty was. With puberty, my whole world would change, and my entire life would collapse into utter despair. I wonder how I would have handled things if I knew."

There was other news in his life. Soumaya was pregnant, and the child was going to be a boy. As much as Elliot didn't feel close to her, he was excited about it and welcomed the thought of a baby brother. He and his sister were not close. Throughout all of Elliot's writing about his life she is barely mentioned.

His parents, as well as Soumaya, had no idea that Elliot was struggling with things as much as he was. To them he just seemed like a quiet and polite boy, one that was just going through normal things that other boys his age went through, albeit maybe in a bit of a more pronounced way. They knew that he struggled with what might be some form of mental illness, and they attempted to get him to counselors and the like to try and help him, but they were proud of him, and loved him, and felt secure he would get through things fine.

Eighth grade started. Elliot continued to be withdrawn and shy, just as he continued to hate those who were more popular than him and did not understand why the pretty girls were drawn to those he felt acted like the biggest jerks. The whole thing was ridiculous to him. What was wrong with the world? Was this what he was supposed to do? Act like an idiot and a fool so a girl would pay attention to him?

Every year was harder. He didn't want to grow up. But yet he had no choice in the matter.

His spent less time with Charlie, John Jo, and Elijah. The sleepovers stopped, and while Elliot was still locked into Planet Cyber, the others began to seem bored with it.

They were moving on to other things and other people. He started to go to Planet Cyber by himself where he would play *Diablo 2* or *World of Warcraft.*

The closest thing to good times Elliot had ever experienced were over. Often he would walk to Planet Cyber by himself thinking of the days gone by. Over time he even started to get bored playing online games; he didn't think that was possible.

One night at Planet Cyber, an older teenager was sitting near Elliot; his screen was easy for Elliot to see. It wasn't that Elliot wanted to notice, but he just couldn't help it. The older boy was watching porn. On the screen, a man was having sex with a woman. He felt traumatized. What was even going on? People do things like this to each other? Was sex really this disgusting? This weird? This angry? He felt a bit aroused, but mostly shocked, guilty, and frightened. He cried for a bit on the walk home.

Later he wrote:

> *This was among the very first glimpses I had of sex. Finding out about sex is one of the things that truly destroyed my entire life. Sex... the very word fills me with hate. Once I hit puberty, I would always want it, like any other boy. I would always hunger for it, I would always covet it, I would always fantasize about it. But I would never get it. Not getting any sex is what will shape the very foundation of my miserable youth. This was a very dark day.*

He couldn't escape it though. There was no place to hide. Boys even started talking about sex at school. Once, a few boys actually told Elliot exactly what happens during sex and how it's done. Elliott had thought things were bad, but they weren't. Now they were. To him, this was the beginning of his true demise.

For the most part, this year was uneventful up until Christmas. Which is when Elliot decided to ask for *World of Warcraft* as his Christmas present from his father.

World of Warcraft is one of the most successful RPG's of all time and is still popular to this day. Some people begin to play *World of Warcraft* and lose hours to the game, while others lose days, weeks, or months. Of course there are many people that just play it here and there for fun, but to others it becomes a lifestyle.

WoW is still considered an excellent game and one that is still quite profitable, back then it was something that, to Elliot, was nothing less than amazing. As he relates:

> *After almost a month went by after getting World of Warcraft, I was finally able to play it. I made a WoW account with my father, and then I created my first character, a night elf druid. It really blew my mind. My first experience with WoW was like stepping into another world of excitement and adventure. It was a video game world, but they made it so realistic that it was like living another life, a more exciting life. My life was getting more and more depressing at that point, and WoW would fill in the void. It felt refreshing and relieving. I was only able to play it for a few hours for my first session. It was all I would think about when I wasn't able to play it.*

He could remember the first day playing as if it was something that happened to him in real life. The emotional memory was that strong. He made his character, choosing it's hair color and different expressions that would be fixed on his face. He was in a forest of brilliant, but soft colors; it had a magical cartoon feeling to it. All around him were other characters, standing, talking, jumping, even laughing.

The realization that all of these people running around are real people, somewhere in the world, in front of their own computers, was mind-blowing to him. All the while there was beautiful delicate and then haunting music playing, while birds were chirping in the trees.

He could see words scrolling on the lower left of his screen, and he soon understood that these were real people, all over the world, talking to one another. They spoke a language he didn't know yet. "LFM Hogger," "Can someone give me 10 silver?" "I can't find the quest giver in the abbey." There were jokes and friendly chatting. He quickly became lost, but it felt good. As if he were exploring a real place, somewhere back in time.

Later he found out he could talk to the other people. Someone asked if he needed help. And soon he had made a friend. They introduced him to other people. Every time he logged on he met new people, discovered a new place, learned new stories from the quest givers, and leveled up. It was addictive.

His mother's computer wasn't good enough to play *WoW* on; his character kept getting stuck, which is known as "lagging"; and it wasn't available at Planet Cyber at the time. For once Elliot was excited to spend more time at his father's house because of *WoW.* Finally they installed the game on all the computers at Planet Cyber. Elliot spent three days checking in there, waiting for it to finally to be ready. He began to spend all his free time there. The owner started to call him his best customer.

His mother moved again; this time into an apartment. Elliot was indignant. He was embarrassed to let anyone know how far his mother had fallen. An apartment was for poor people in his eyes. He stopped seeing what few friends he had there, as he didn't want any of them to know where he lived. On the last day at his mother's house he cried.

He never again hung out with Charlie, John Jo, and Elijah. They were gone and not his friends anymore. His only friend was James. His mother did get better Internet at least, so he could play *WoW* at her home. Even though it was the type of place he was embarrassed to be seen at, he could at least have some pleasure while he was there.

What little social life he had was gone. He was lonely, only connecting with people through games, other than James on occasion, but even that was mostly online. It wasn't that he was actually doing anything to make friends, but that didn't make him feel any better about his lot in life.

He became very depressed. He stopped trying to be cool. He just played *WoW* and lived in a world where he felt safe. In his opinion, he had given everything his best shot; he had tried his hardest. What more could he do?

He spent just about all of his free time playing the game. To Elliot, school was just something that took his time away from *WoW*. He leveled his toon, which is another name for a *World of Warcraft* character, geared him up, went on raids, worked on his skills and talents. The thing about *World of Warcraft* is there is truly no end to it, there is always something to do, something to achieve, and to Elliot, who was achieving nothing in his real life, it was intoxicating.

When he was at school he was still mostly the quiet kid, but occasionally he started to act bizarre just so he wasn't invisible all the time. At least if he acted odd, he knew he was seen.

So now he wasn't the shy kid anymore, he was the weird kid. This didn't bother him too much as he had ceased to care what the other boys thought of him. In his mind they were just fools anyway, but then a cadre of popular girls started to tease him as well. This hurt so much. He couldn't understand why people were so cruel to him. As Elliot wrote: "I started to hate all girls because of this. I saw them as mean, cruel, and heartless creatures that took pleasure from my suffering."

Elliot was happy when his brother Jazz was born. He looked forward to being a big brother, and spending time with Jazz, maybe even letting him know what life was truly about.

Still, *WoW* was his number one priority. At his father's house, there were many limits as to how much time he could spend playing the game. It made Elliot angry that Soumaya just wouldn't mind her own business and leave him alone. But, when at his mother's, he could play as much as he wanted to. When spring break came, he spent his entire week playing the game.

James came over to the apartment one day, for he was the only person Elliot had ever invited there, the only person he trusted enough not to mock him for how far he felt his mother had fallen. He introduced him to the wonders of *WoW* and was pleased James seemed interested. It made him feel validated somehow.

School continued to get worse. Instead of being invisible Elliot was now weird and incredibly unpopular. He hated to be teased, mocked, and bullied, but at least he was being noticed. He started getting a rush by picking fights with the popular kids and winding them up. He was angry, miserable, and depressed.

His parents continued to try to get him help, but they had no idea what was really going on in Elliot's mind. Around this time he was diagnosed with "Pervasive Development Disorder – Not Otherwise Specified," which is one of a group of disorders characterized by delays in the development of socialization and communication skills. It is used by mental health professionals to describe people who don't fit neatly into one of the specific kinds of autism, such as autistic disorder, Asperger syndrome, or childhood disintegrative disorder.

He was still very shy in public and had difficulty doing the types of things other kids would do. Even buying something in a store without the assistance of his parents was difficult for him.

There was one girl he had a crush on. He thought he might be deeply in love with her although he never admitted it to anyone. Elliot felt that in a fair and just world, if you love someone then soon they might love you back as long as you treated them well, and Elliot certainly did. But she made fun of him too. It hurt him so much when she teased him. It broke his heart. So he played more *WoW* to shelter himself from the storm.

The summer finally came. High school was looming. As much as Elliot hated middle school he had no doubt whatsoever that high school would be much worse. Each year more was expected of him to fit in, and each year he felt he never lived up to what society thought he should be. He still couldn't figure it out. He thought he was intelligent, interesting, refined, and not bad looking at all, but yet his life continued to be torture.

He buried himself in *WoW* for the summer, trying to avoid any thought of what high school might be like. Just as when he started middle school, what bothered him most was the thought of having to be around girls. He worried they'd be mean to him. They would ignore him, or even worse, mock him. When he started middle school the expectation was that Elliot might be expected to kiss a girl, now he might be expected to have sex with one. He was terrified.

There was only one solution. He begged his parents to send him to Crespi Carmelite High School, a private Roman Catholic boys' school in Encino. He thought that might help him avoid the pain. Perhaps he would fit in better there. It was a prestigious school, so his parents were amenable; they were even pleased he was attempting to apply himself. Elliot submitted an application, which was accepted.

At the graduation ceremony for eighth graders, Elliot and the rest of the students went up on stage, announced their names, and said where they were going to be attending high school. There was a large crowd there, including his parents, Soumaya, and his sister and brother. As Elliot got in line to get on stage he began to shake and tremble. When it was his turn, he walked on stage with his knees shaking and his heart in his chest and said, "My name is Elliot, and I plan on going to Crespi High School."

His family acted as if they were proud of him later that night. He thought they were ridiculous. Elliot wasn't proud. He believed everything had turned out horribly, and he was a disappointment to them.

Elliot's plan was simple for the summer. He would play *WoW,* which is what he did. He joined a guild, which is a group of people on a server who do things like organize raids together and help each other with quests. He leveled up his character as far as it could go. He considered this to be important. Sometimes he would play for eight to ten hours a day.

But after just a few weeks of summer, his father told him that he was going to Morocco with them for eight weeks. Elliot freaked out. He didn't like Morocco. It was like stepping back in time. He hated it there. They didn't have the right video games, and he wouldn't be able to play *WoW* at all. It was a nightmare.

His summer was a disaster: then it was time for school.

A WORTHLESS
LITTLE MOUSE

Things went worse than he possibly could have imagined. He was bullied the very first week at Crespi. Some seniors picked on him because he was small and weak. They could sense a wounded animal in their midst, and while at Crespi, Elliot's wounds only grew deeper. They threw food at him during lunch, and even when school ended, they would taunt him while he waited to go home.

Elliot felt anger growing inside of him, but didn't dare to fight back. In his mind, he was too small, too alone, like there was nothing he could do. He felt too weak.

He went further into the thought process that people were truly horrible. People are monsters.

He decided to stop doing his homework and spend more time on *WoW*. What was the point? Soumaya often gave him a hard time about how much time he spent playing the game, but, as he was so often in his room on his laptop, no one really knew exactly how much time he played. He was good at keeping secrets.

Elliot found that his only friend James was now regularly playing *WoW* as well. This gave him some solace and reminded him of the days when he was a child, when things were simpler. At least he had one person who understood him.

Things got worse at school. He made a point to let people know how much he despised skateboarding, which was true because in his mind he had failed at it, so of course, he hated it. Because of this, kids kept calling him a "skateboarder." This just made him very angry, which of course caused his tormenters to call him that even more. Soon he was being called "Faggot." Some kids would take his things away from him, so he would get angry and chase after them, which they thought was hilarious. He felt too weak to do anything about it. He would hide in a corner of the hallway until they were mostly empty then walk to class so he wouldn't be bullied.

Finally it was time for winter vacation. A break from the torture, some of which was self-imposed, some not. Elliot was so happy that he was away from school. All he wanted to do was play *WoW* and hide, but Soumaya continued to harass him about the amount of time he spent playing the game and began to limit the time he spent playing it each day. He started to hate her with his whole being. He couldn't understand. This was the only thing he had that gave him any joy, and she wanted him to do it less? She wanted him to be more unhappy?

Puberty came for Elliot despite his protestations and with it came sexual urges. To his great dismay, he began to get so worked up that he started to rub himself against his mattress at night. The first time he came it was an accident. He was shocked. He simply couldn't believe how good it made him feel. This started to be something he did often, his masturbating becoming more pronounced as the days went on. One might think it brought him some relief, but in fact the opposite was true. It made things worse. Now he knew he wanted to have sex; he knew how good it would feel to orgasm with a beautiful woman, and he knew he wouldn't have it. He began to think he would never actually have sex. And he was right. He never did.

He felt that he was totally alone in this. As he wrote:

> *The boys in my grade talked about sex a lot.*
> *Some of them even told me that they had sex with*

*their girlfriends. This was the most devastating
and traumatizing thing I've ever heard in my life.
Boys having sex at my age of fourteen? I couldn't
fathom it. How is it that they were able to have such
intimate and pleasurable experiences with girls
while I could only fantasize about it? I frequently
started asking myself. This was an all-boys'
school... How in the hell were those boys even
able to meet girls to have sex with? I wondered.
I hoped they were lying. I hoped against all hope.
Hearing that really shook me to the core. Words
cannot describe how much hatred and envy I felt
for those boys. That hatred would only fester the
more I suffer from my sexual starvation. I was too
scared to tell anyone about it, and I hid it well...
for a time.*

Isolation continued to be his friend. When he was by himself,
it was the only time he felt safe. All he did was hang out in
his room and play *World of Warcraft;* it remained the most
important thing in his life. He joined a better guild where
they would raid for hours on end; sometimes he would stay
up all night playing. He was good in the game at least, but
still not as good as some others who put even less time in
than he did. To his dismay he wasn't even all that good at
his obsession. He stopped doing homework, and his grades
suffered, but he could care less.

School was a nightmare. Every day he felt terrified, like
a tiny worthless, mouse. He cried every day. One afternoon
his mother had to get him at school because he had a panic
attack; he stood in the hallway, frozen like a statue, afraid to
move. He cried all the way home in her car. He never went
back to Crespi again.

At first he felt that he might be safe now that he was gone
from Crespi, that things could get better, but then his parents
told him they were sending him to a school named Taft,

a public high school in Woodland Hills with many more students than Crespi and even worse, one that was filled with girls. Elliot felt like his parents had stabbed him in the back. While his father later said that Elliot never talked to him about what was really going on inside his mind and that he didn't know the extent of Elliot's fear, Elliot knew it would be even worse at Taft than at Crespi. And worse, he felt abandoned by those he thought of as his protectors because in his mind they didn't know or care how afraid he was, or how much he suffered. He felt they were throwing him to wolves.

When he went to orientation at Taft, he was terrified by what he saw. The school was enormous. All the students were so tall that they looked like giants. He worried they would eat him alive. He begged his parents to send him back to Crespi, but to no avail.

The first day at Taft was a nightmare. His father had to physically drag him out of the car because he was so terrified that he refused to get out. He got lost almost immediately. During break from class he hid in a corner of a hallway because of his fear. It never got better. The bullying was much worse than Crespi ever was. He felt like a mouse thrown into a pit of snakes.

As he wrote:

> *I was completely and utterly alone. No one knew me or extended a hand to help me. I was an innocent, scared little boy trapped in a jungle full of malicious predators, and I was shown no mercy. Some boys randomly pushed me against the lockers as they walked past me in the hall. One boy who was tall and had blonde hair called me a "loser," right in front of his girlfriends. Yes, he had girls with him. Pretty girls. And they didn't seem to mind that he was such an evil bastard. In fact, I bet they liked him for it. This is how girls are,*

and I was starting to realize it. This was what truly opened my eyes to how brutal the world is. The most meanest and depraved of men come out on top, and women flock to these men. Their evil acts are rewarded by women; while the good, decent men are laughed at. It is sick, twisted, and wrong in every way. I hated the girls even more than the bullies because of this. The sheer cruelty of the world around me was so intense that I will never recover from the mental scars. Any experience I ever had before never traumatized me as much as this.

Elliot couldn't take anymore and broke down completely. Day after day he literally begged his parents, crying and shaking, to not make him go to school anymore. After a week or so of this they took him out of Taft.

For a month, Elliot stayed at home licking his wounds. He wasn't happy to be alone, at home with no friends, but at least he felt safe from predators and humiliation. His parents decided to enroll him at Independence Continuation High School, which had just 100 students and was designed to help children that had a difficult time functioning in a normal school environment for a variety of reasons.

At Independence, it was later reported that he needed reassurance from the teacher about five to ten times per day. He was able to socialize if other students sought him out, but he didn't approach others.

The teachers were kind to him, and so were most of the students although he didn't like most of them as he thought they were "slobs." This was Elliot's vibe his entire life. He was desperate to fit it with the cool crowd and was angered by how they treated him, or even worse, ignored him. Yet when he came into contact with anyone, he thought they were beneath him in social status, intelligence, or appearance. He wanted nothing to do with them.

He didn't want friends anymore anyway. It was way too much pressure for him to deal with. The workload at his new school was easily manageable; they didn't expect much from him. He went to school for part of the morning, was left alone by the other students, then went home to play *WoW*. He wasn't picked on, in fact, some of the students were even protective of him although he barely spoke to any of them. Some staff members found him endearing and referred to him amongst themselves as "our Elliot."

Peter had started to direct his own self-funded documentary, *"Oh My God?,"* a movie in which he traveled the world asking people, famous and not, the question "What is God?" He had invested a lot of his time and most of his money into it. Because of this, he was gone often, which left Elliot alone with Soumaya much more than he would like. One can imagine Soumaya felt the same way, neither were big fans of each other at this point.

Soumaya continued to try to limit Elliot's time on *WoW*, which frustrated and angered him. He wanted her to just leave him alone. Still, Elliot had hope for his father's movie. There was much talk of how successful it might be and how much money would be made from it. If his father became rich from this, Elliot thought it could benefit him greatly when it came to his social status. He felt it would be much easier for him to be popular and to meet girls if he were rich and famous.

It turned out to be a colossal flop but offered hope at the time. The movie received only 22 percent on the movie review site Rotten Tomatoes and didn't even come close to making what Peter had spent on it. Worse, it was thought of as vapid and uninspired. Peter Rodger had set out to make a movie that would make the world think, but he had massively overestimated his ability to do so.

Over the winter of 2007, a new expansion of *WoW*, "Burning Crusade," came out. Elliot was thrilled. He transferred his toon to the same server that James was on and also met a couple of James's friends, Steve and Mark, that James played *WoW* with. It was a whole new world for him to live in and explore. As always, it was one that he enjoyed much more than the real one. Elliot had fun playing with these three. They were friends that he did something with on a regular basis, even if he didn't see them all that often in the real world.

But Soumaya continued to not get the whole *World of Warcraft* thing. To Elliot it was like she wanted him to be miserable. They began to fight constantly about Elliot playing *WoW.* His room was right across from hers, and she knew, or at least suspected, how much time he spent playing the game, and she wasn't having it. She often asked him to do chores, and if he refused, sometimes she took his laptop away for a day or two. To Elliot this was beyond cruel. It was the only thing that made him happy. He couldn't understand why she tried stopping him from having any kind of joy in his life.

There was one other thing that he enjoyed doing though, masturbating. His fantasies were rather vanilla. He would think of a hot blonde woman and imagine that she was his girlfriend, then he'd picture the two of them having sex. That was pretty much it. Elliot didn't have any dark or odd sexual fantasies. He had no fetishes or kinks. He just wanted to have sex with someone beautiful and to have her look adoringly in his eyes while he made sweet love to her.

One night Elliott and his family were invited to a dinner party thrown by Peter's friends. There were some other teenagers there. They were good looking; they were cool. They began talking about parties they went to, their social lives, their dating lives, things such as that. Elliot broke down. He cried. He talked of killing himself in front of everyone because he felt he would never have a life like theirs.

Summer break came. Eleventh grade was over, and he had just one more year to go before he was free, an adult.

School meant nothing to him. He went to school, didn't talk to anyone, did what he had to do to survive, then got on the bus and went home. He took the bus to school even though it embarrassed him, as he didn't feel like he was old enough to drive. He still thought of himself as a child, and children didn't drive cars. He was becoming more depressed by the day.

As he wrote:

> *It was at this time that I was just beginning to realize, with a lot of clarity, how truly unfair my life is. I compared myself to other teenagers and became very angry that they were able to experience all of the things I've desired, while I was left out of it. I never had the experience of going to a party with other teenagers, I never had my first kiss, I never held hands with a girl, I never lost my virginity. In the past, I felt so inferior and weak from all of the bullying that I just accepted my lonely life and dealt with it by playing WoW, but at this point I started to question why I was condemned to suffer such misery. There was nothing I could really do about my unfair life situation. I felt completely powerless.*

His senior year began. Elliot was allowed to work at his own pace and was determined to graduate early, so he could be done with high school for good. Even though he wasn't picked on at Independence, the other students at his school disgusted him. He thought they were low class and stupid and beneath him. He felt he was wasting his time being at this school every day. Elliot continued to chastise those above him on the social totem pole while at the same time mocking those he considered beneath him. The irony of this was totally lost on him.

Another *WoW* expansion, "Wrath of the Lich King," dropped. He walked nearly an hour to BestBuy to get the game as soon as it came out. He continued to play *WoW* with the closest thing he had to friends, James, Steve, and Mark, but even in this social circle, he was the outcast. The others met to play at one of their houses often, but Elliot was never invited. Sometimes he would be playing with them online only to find to his horror the others were all in the same room playing together in the real world without having invited him. This made him angry, but he didn't dare to say anything about it, lest he lose his only friends.

Elliot became even more lonely, and the more alone he felt the angrier he became. Even *WoW* stopped making him feel happy. He often sobbed while playing the game. He resolved to play it less; it wasn't helping anymore.

Around this time he was prescribed Xanax and Prozac, but he only took these medications regularly for a short time. He also took Paxil as needed, for instance, if he was going to a party with his family or any sort of social event. In a journal entry, Elliot wrote that the pills made him feel too drowsy and tired, so he decided he would stop taking them and would "have to rely entirely on my mind and positive thinking" to overcome his shyness.

It seemed impossible that a girl would ever want to date him, let alone have sex with him. And what was worse, he simply couldn't figure out why.

He began to become even more angry towards anyone who was having sex, or even the fact girls seemed to desire it. He considered himself at war with those that had sex. The line had been drawn in the sand. He was lonely and miserable, while other boys lived like kings. To him, sex was the reason everything was bad in the world. He had been hiding from the world like a loser, but now he decided it was time to fight back. The anger made him feel strong. It was a new feeling. He liked that.

He started to fantasize about being all powerful. If he could not have sex, he would stop others from having it as well. Sex should be a crime. If it wasn't available to Elliot, then no one would be able to have it. Yes, he believed his life was ruined. But that didn't mean he was nothing. He thought he was incredibly intelligent, and not only that, he could see the world in a way that most couldn't. He began to think his destiny was to change the world. Maybe that was why these challenges were put before him.

He opened up to James and told him that he believed that sex should be outlawed. He was pleased that James seemed to understand his viewpoints on the matter.

Meanwhile, Peter's documentary *Oh My God?* was finally released. The movie cost around $1,000,000 to film, which isn't all that much in the grand scheme of things, but it made only around $38,000 back. It was a flop. It only was shown in a few theaters and was poorly reviewed. Peter was embarrassed, and worse he was a bit broke.

This upset Elliot even more. His thought process at the time went something like this. All that he was dealing with and now he wasn't even rich? His dad wasn't to become famous, instead he became a joke. Instead of being the son of a man who made a blockbuster movie, he was the son of a failure. He thought his father was strong and impressive, but instead he was a fool. Elliot would never meet a woman.

Still, Elliot had something to live for. He wrote:

> *I formed an ideology in my head of how the world should work. I was fueled both by my desire to destroy all of the injustices of the world, and to exact revenge on everyone I envy and hate. I decided that my destiny in life is to rise to power so I can impose my ideology on the world and set everything right. I was only seventeen, I have plenty of time. I thought to myself. I spent all of my time studying in my room, reading books about history, politics, and sociology, trying to learn as much as I can. I became a new person, furiously*

driven by a goal. My torment would continue, but I
had something to live for. I felt empowered.

He talked more to James about how much he thought sex should be outlawed and discovered James didn't understand his ideas nearly as much as Elliot thought. James replied that the only reason Elliot didn't want others to have sex is that he couldn't get laid himself. Elliot admitted that he was right, but to him that still didn't change the basic premise of how unjust everything was. It was surprising to him that James didn't see this.

Elliot got all his work done and finished high school early, in February. As much as he was happy to be finally through with that Hell, it just gave him more time to ruminate and perseverate on his life, or lack of one.

INCEL CULTURE

It isn't easy to be a virgin. It can mess with your mind.

Once a person gets that issue over with, once one has sex with even one woman, or one man, as the case may be, the monkey is off one's back. The person has moved from the club of the undesired, to the other and their life has changed forever. It's the kind of thing that, in today's society, can really eat away at one's self-esteem. Especially if one is lacking in that area in the first place.

Of course some remain virgins for moral reasons. Some never have sex by choice. They want to save themselves for marriage, or maybe to be in love. Other times, one might be a virgin for more complicated reasons such as trauma, but, even then, that is the classic "It's not you, it's me scenario." One might have issues about the trauma itself but not about being a virgin.

But, imagine a person who wants to have sex and, for whatever reason, no one seems to want to have sex with them? Now in the case of Elliot Rodger, this doesn't quite hold up. He constantly said no one wanted him, but he also would never even consider going out with someone that wasn't totally gorgeous, or immensely desirable.

In his entire tome, or manifesto, he never seemed to entertain the thought of dating a girl or a woman who might be a bit on the shy side, that might be cute, but not gorgeous. Possibly he could have found a young woman that really liked to play *WoW* for example, that might be a bit of a nerd perhaps. But he would never consider such a thing. He thought he deserved so much more.

He didn't have female friends, in fact it doesn't seem like he ever even got to know a female, or even tried to. This is what makes Elliot Rodger such a complicated character. In some ways he is incredibly sympathetic. In other ways, not so much at all.

Not only that, but despite all his protestations, it appears that he never attempted to get to know a woman, or a girl for that matter, in any real way. He simply would walk by some girls he wanted to impress, look at them, and expect them to fall at his feet. He would put himself in situations, by wearing the right clothes, or driving the right car, or even trying to go to the right party, all to try and meet someone of the opposite sex. But he never once actually asked anyone out, or even really got to know any female in any way, over the course of his entire life.

But still, when one is single and not celibate by choice, it matters and it hurts. In one's mind, a person might think everyone else but them is having sex, and because of that there is something drastically wrong with them. Or in Elliot's case, thinking that everyone else but him is having sex, which means there is something drastically wrong with the rest of the world.

If a person is involuntarily celibate, it's like they don't exist to the opposite sex, or maybe they do exist and others simply don't desire them. But even if one is in that situation, does that mean sex is owed to them? That they deserve it?

Check out Bumble, Tinder, and Grindr. Sure, there might be a bit about personality involved, or at least about knowing the right thing to type on a screen to make them look attractive, but basically they're, in theory, hooking up with people who are just into their looks, and nothing else. If they're not getting any hits, what is it? Are they too short? Too fat? Do they have bad hair, are they ugly? Maybe they dress badly?

A significant percentage of men blame women when they feel bad about their dating prospects. These types think women don't want the nice guy, the good guy. They just want a jerk with money or a good body that treats them poorly.

So then we have the incels. A group of men who are positive that attractive women don't want them. As a group they exist almost entirely online. They mostly cluster together on the Internet and bemoan their lot in life, joining together to support each other through this awful situation. Of course, many of them, just like Elliot, would never dream of reaching out to an average looking woman to have sex with, or even a relationship with. To them it would be embarrassing to be with a woman who wasn't perfect looking.

Just what is an incel? It depends on who is asked. The basic definition is people who are unable to find a sexual partner despite desiring to do so. Of course, most so-called incels don't belong to any group at all; they just do their own thing. As far as those who band together on the Internet, some of them are quite innocuous, simply people looking for a support group, so they can talk about their lives with likeminded people who understand them.

Others, not so much. The Southern Poverty Law Center calls incels "online male supremacists" and classifies them as a hate group. The vast majority are male and heterosexual.

Incels often think they're ugly, or short, or something else they consider awful and as such they can't have sex with anyone. No matter how much they try to change their outlook, or their game, or their appearance by working out or getting a cool haircut, they still don't think they have a chance in Hell to succeed with women. This is because to them, women are shallow fools who only care about looks and will see through any attempt of a man to try to improve.

Now this is where it gets tricky though because obviously all incels are not like what follows. Despite what many people might think or believe, it would be ridiculous to even imply that.

But some incels believe, and many pretend to believe, that they should be able to have sex with pretty much any woman they want, without her having any input about it. They should make this choice, not women. Women are worthless unless on their backs or on their knees. Of course many of these types don't understand that this attitude is much more the reason they never get laid as opposed to their looks.

Incels don't have it easy. They are often made fun of, either because they're guys that can't have sex, or because they're considered threats to society in general. Quite often they are individuals who are isolated, depressed, and lack self-esteem, and this image doesn't help those issues.

Since Elliot Rodger's rampage, other men, who in the media have been described as incels, have committed mass murders. The media have criticized incel communities for being misogynistic and encouraging violence, and much of the public believes this to be true.

While it is often thought that not having sex is the main aspect of being an incel, some in the community say that sex is not the real issue and that an incel could be anyone that wants to find love and be in a relationship and has been unable to do so. Most incels feel that it is much easier for a female, or even a homosexual man, to have sex than it is for a heterosexual man.

Incels use a lot of slang, some of which will be covered later in this chapter, but even if one is in the fringes of what incel culture is all about, one has to know the difference between the blue pill, red pill, and black pill, the names of which are derived from the movie *The Matrix*.

Those who take the blue pill are what most people might consider to have an optimistic, or even somewhat normal, point of view. They feel that if one has a good personality and is true to whom one is, the person in question should have no problem hooking up with a woman even if they aren't totally good looking.

Those who take the red pill believe that while appearance is important there are also a lot of things that can be done to be successful with the opposite sex. If one works on one's pick-up game, acts in a charming manner, dresses well, goes to the gym and works out and so on, one can do well with the opposite sex even if not blessed with good looks or natural charm.

Incels are all about the black pill. If good looking, one is always going to do better with a woman than if just having a good personality. The more unattractive one is, the less chance of finding someone. In fact there might even be no chance at all. The world is totally stacked against men who don't have the right genes, and women are always going to want men that have certain facial features, bone structure, and body type, oh and of course money.

While Elliot Rodger may not have had the Day of Retribution that he sought, he certainly wound up having a lot of influence. The word "Incel" was heard by most for the first time after his killings, although it has been around since 1997 when visual artist Alana Boltwood started an online support group called "Alana's Involuntary Celibacy Project." It was later shortened to incel.

At first, incel groups were considered support groups of a sort, the same way an online AA group would work. People would get together online and chat about their difficulties being involuntarily celibate. But there is no denying that over time things have become quite a bit more intense in such forums.

In any online forum, there are numerous people saying the most messed up things they can think of just to mess with people. Trolling used to be something used as an insult, and it still is, but now quite often it is thought of as an artform in certain circles.

Incel culture takes this to a new extreme. The most popular incel forum today is Incels.Is. As of this book's writing ,a sampling of thread titles on this forum are "Height > Face," "I cum in Foid's roommates shower gel," and "Why I support the Legalization of Rape."

One person on the forum writes: "Why even leave the house just being around people will make you despise yourself even more. It's an extremely lonely feeling to be around a bunch of people that couldn't give zero fucks about your livelihood, especially the foids that see us as beneath them... they'll give you looks of disgust and treat you like absolutely shit... Humans are just pure sociopaths and evil in general."

The thread titled "Why I support the Legalization of rape" opines:

> First, it is scientifically proven that women are more likely to experience an orgasm during rape. Second, rapists are responding to a demand by women to fulfill their rape fantasies. Third, women feel sexually aroused by the fact a rapist is willing to risk jail to help himself to her pussy. Fourth, raping women is the correct thing to do. There are countless verses in the Qur'an which basically say it is the divine right of a husband to rape his wife is she doesn't fuck him when he wants. Fifth, it pisses off normies, soycucks and feminists. So what is there not to like about legalized rape? Sixth, it will solve the inceldom crisis. It is for these reasons that I support the legalization of rape.

One commenter in this thread said: "Foids must be culled. We should be the selectors and the mentors of our offspring. Foids are but a vessel."

When you look at people writing such vile words, whether you're terrified or feel you're in the comfort of expert trolls, completely depends on your worldview. Are these people dangerous? Or are they just dudes on the Internet messing with the world and each other in a space they consider safe. What if it is a little of both?

Some are just sad. In one thread titled "My mom says I do the virgin walk," a member wrote: "She said I walk like a penguin. That's what I actually thought to myself a few days ago when I saw my reflection while walking, but she fucking confirmed it today. Add that to my ever growing list of insecurities. So fucking over."

Incels.Is is hosted out of Iceland. It used to be found at Incels.me until its website host shut it down saying it was "suspended over anti-abuse policy infractions based on the promotion of acts of violence and hate speech on the website."

The site's owner and administrator, who goes by "Serge" told me:

> *We are starting to touch upon the topic of freedom of speech. I have personally very strong views regarding this which doesn't necessarily have to do with inceldom, but I'll explain here: We live in an ever increasing state of totalitarianism in our society, where politically correct speech is being enforced constantly, and people who are seen as controversial or as a liability in terms of public relationships have their accounts terminated or are banned. In our case, the .me domain registrar terminated our domain, despite the fact we host no illegal discussion of any kind and that we had been with them for a year already. So what happened? We started to become more known. Thus, the company decided to cut us off in order to stop people from adding negative connotations to the .me address.*

The site came into existence in part when Reddit banned a group of incels who were 40,000 strong because the group "encourages, glorifies, incites or calls for violence or physical harm against an individual or group of people." The rules of the subreddit didn't ban women but said: "Those who continuously claim there are as many female incels in the same situation as male incels will receive a warning and then a ban. Most can agree that women can be incel in some rare situations such as extreme disfigurement, but their numbers do not come close to male incels."

A tipping point was when a male member of the group was caught pretending to be a woman asking for advice on how rapists were caught. In other words, asking for advice on how to get away with rape.

Most groups formed online have their own slang and lexicon, but incels take it to another level. They often use symbology in their communication. What follows is some of the most prevalent online terms they use. One needs to know the terms to have an idea of what they're writing about.

Beta

When it comes to wolves, an alpha is the leader of the pack, the wolf that is the strongest, and gets the most attention. To an incel, pick-up artists, popular guys, and jocks are undeniably the alphas of the male race while they are nothing but betas, which is a lower ranking wolf in the pack. A beta isn't charming. A beta runs when confronted by a tougher man. Some incels call themselves an "Omega," which are literally the lowest ranking wolf of all.

Chad

Chad is a guy that is everything that an incel is not. He is handsome, charming, confident, and hooks up with women easily. While a typical incel hates Chads, they also tend to worship the ground they walk on. Even if an incel gets lucky enough to hook up with a woman, and maybe even get a girlfriend, sooner or later Chad will steal her away from him.

Black Pill

The origin of this term is from the movie *The Matrix*. To take the black pill is to admit that what women really want is a good looking man with certain facial features and body type. No amount of charm, intelligence, or pick-up artist techniques will help alter the fact that if they aren't good looking, women will never want them. In fact, incels should just give up and stop trying to be successful with women. In essence, incels who take the black pill have zero hope, the world is simply stacked against them because of their inferior looks and body type and there is nothing they can do about it.

Blue Pill

To take the blue pill is to think that everything is fair in life, and that hot women and good looking men don't have unfair advantages over the rest of the male herd. If one is an incel, this is considered just falling for an illusion and seeing things that aren't real.

Cope

To take the black pill is to admit that there is literally nothing they can do as an incel to have more success with women. Therefore, anything that they might attempt to do is a "cope." In other words, a temporary way to make themselves feel better. Going to college, getting a cool haircut, working out at the gym, driving a nice car, are all copes, and none of them will help an incel get laid or find a girlfriend.

Cuck

A cuck is traditionally known as a man whose wife or girlfriend is having sex with another man. Sometimes the humiliated man even gets off on it. This means the same to incels, but is used much more often as slang for almost any situation where an incel is happily dominated by a Chad.

E.R.

This stands for the man himself, Elliot Rodger.

Femoid or Foid

This is a common term for women when it comes to incel slang and stands for "female humanoid."

Gymcel

Just as it sounds, a Gymcel is an incel who goes to the gym a lot, which in their mind is a cope. If one is an incel, no matter how much one tries to build up the body, it will still never work; one is still an incel.

Heightcel

This is someone who is an incel because they're short. To a true incel someone who is tall and is still not getting any sort of dates or sexual activity is just someone who is voluntarily celibate.

It's Over

This is the true incel creed. It is often followed by the phrase "It never began." This is what the black pill is truly all about.

MGTOW

This stands for Men Going Their Own Way. They claim to not want to have anything to do with women in any way whatsoever. These men aren't quite incels, as they simply don't want to be with women.

MOG

This means to be dominated and surpassed by another man. One could be heightmogged by someone taller, or voicemogged by someone with a deeper voice. Elliot Rodger mogs pretty much everyone. The origins are the term AMOG, which stands for "Alpha Male of the Group."

Normie

This term pretty much stands for anyone who is average in looks, outlook on life, and intelligence. Some incels use this as an insult while others would love to be a normie, even though it's obvious to all incels that the worldview of a normie is lacking.

Race> Height > Face > Money

Serge of Incels.is says of this: "This is a bit of a debatable topic in the incel community. It simply goes that your race is more important when trying to get relationships than your height, which is more important than your facial appearance, which is more important than how wealthy you are. Some incels disagree on the order of these things, some disagree they should be put in such a chain at all, some consider them all equally important."

Red Pill

To take the red pill is to recognize that the world is unfair and that women have all the power and hold all the cards. But, red pillers think that one can actually *become* an Alpha male by doing things like hitting the gym, using pick-up artist techniques, and treating women like dogs. True Incels don't buy into this.

Rope

When an incel talks about roping themselves, it means to kill themselves, to end it all. It is often used in a flippant manner.

Stacy

Stacys are women who are hot, dumb, and like to have sex a lot. But they only want to have sex with Chads and would never do it with an incel.

Volcel

This is someone who is voluntarily celibate. To an incel, these people are to be mocked and shunned. Not many things are more irritating than a guy who actually "could" have sex or even will in the future and is acting like he is a true incel.

Wristcel

Someone who is an incel because they have tiny wrists, which of course doom them to never have sex.

As odd, and even as amusing, as some of this terminology might be, those who identify with the "Involuntary Celibate" movement are thought of more and more as domestic terrorism threats.

A report done in early 2020 by the Texas Department of Public Safety titled the "Texas Domestic Terrorism Threat" opines:

> *Although not a new movement, Involuntary Celibates (Incels) are an emerging domestic terrorism threat as current adherents demonstrate marked acts or threats of violence in furtherance of their social grievance. Once viewed as a criminal threat by many law enforcement authorities, Incels are now seen as a growing domestic terrorism concern due to the ideological nature of recent Incel attacks internationally, nationwide, and in Texas.*

The report goes on to say: "What begins as a personal grievance due to perceived rejection by women may morph into allegiance to, and attempts to further, an Incel Rebellion. The result has thrust the Incel movement into the realm of domestic terrorism," The report explained. "The violence demonstrated by Incels in the past decade, coupled with extremely violent online rhetoric, suggests this particular threat could soon match, or potentially eclipse, the level of lethalness demonstrated by other domestic terrorism types."

ALPHA DOG

Things seemed hopeless. Sure, Elliot Rodger had decided that he wanted to rise to power, and if he could do so he thought that he would be happy, but how exactly would he do so? It wasn't like it was something that was easy to accomplish. Many men have tried to rise to power and failed. Was he just being ridiculous? He certainly hoped not.

As he had nothing to fill up his time, he began to take long walks around town, or he would go to the mall and hang out. Every time he saw a couple holding hands, making out, or even looking content while together, he felt a white-hot anger deep inside his body. One that continued to grow.

His parents were becoming worried that he was doing nothing with himself, so they decided to send Elliot to Morocco with Soumaya for a few months. This surprised Elliot and angered him greatly. He couldn't understand what they were thinking. His parents solution to his misery was to send him to Morocco, a place he truly despised? He thought of it barely above a Third World country. He would be even more bored there than he was in America, even more alone. His mind reeled. It was bad enough they didn't understand him, did they have to torture him too? Morocco with Soumaya? It made him shudder to think of it.

He wasn't going to let this happen. A ticket had been purchased for him, and they were supposed to leave within five days. He threw a tantrum to show his displeasure, the biggest one he could muster, but that accomplished nothing, so instead he decided to pretend to be okay with it all and made a plan to escape. He decided the best way to accomplish this was to run away on the morning of the flight, walk to his mother's house, and hide on the roof. He would emerge once Soumaya was gone and deal with the fallout later. Not the best of plans, but Elliot's plans were always a little muddled.

When the fateful day came, he got up at 4 a.m. to make his escape, but apparently his father was aware something odd might happen and had set an alarm on the door. Even if he got out, his father would be right after him. He decided his best course of action was to wait until breakfast time then make a run for it. He told his father he wanted to take a bit of a walk, just a short one. He acted as if he was happy to go on the trip; he was even looking forward to it. As soon as he got through the door, he ran like crazy. His escape attempt was doomed from the start. As soon as he began his mad dash, he turned around and saw Peter chasing after him. He gave up almost immediately. He could never outrun Peter, his legs were too short. He was going to Morocco.

It didn't go well. As Elliot wrote :

> *The journey to Morocco was the most horrendous travel experience I've ever had. It was just me, Soumaya, and four-year-old Jazz. Jazz kept screaming and vomiting on the plane, Soumaya was in a sour mood, and I was completely miserable. I thought my whole life was all over. I had nothing to look forward to in the future. I wanted to die. Once I got there, I felt like all of the life in me had drained out. I was so defeated. I couldn't help but cry all the time, even in front of Soumaya's relatives. Khadija (Elliot's grandmother) didn't understand why I was so upset, and she got offended that I was crying on the first day at her house. It was a complete disaster.*

One must remember that Elliot, who is crying hysterically all the time, is 17 years old. He constantly emailed his mother from overseas, begging for another chance, that he would lead a good life, that he would try harder. He would find a job, he would go to college, he would do anything she wanted him to. He told her that he couldn't stop crying, that he was miserable. After a week of this constant onslaught his mother flew to Morocco to bring him home.

He was happy when he got back home to his mother's house. For a few days at least. Then he remembered who he was; he remembered his hate and sadness.

He continued to spend time walking around town or at the mall, but when he did he'd feel intense hate towards any happy couple he saw. He constantly fantasized about being powerful, about punishing those that he despised. He was living almost completely in his head at this point, and it was not a pleasant place for Elliot to be.

One day when he was riding his bike around aimlessly, some teenagers in an SUV drove past and mocked him. He assumed it was because of his clothing and because he was riding a bike at his age. He was wearing a polo shirt and khaki pants, which in Elliot's mind made him look like a loser. Like many experiences that Elliot had, this stayed with him, he thought of it often. It rattled around in his brain.

No one understood what was going on with him. His father thought he was fine. He thought of him as a nice polite boy; one that wouldn't harm a flea. Elliot felt his father had failed him for never teaching him how to meet girls, or helped him prepare for the world, and who never warned him how awful his life would be if he didn't attract women. His father thought him fine, when in reality Elliot would sit in his room and cry for hours.

Elliot decided it was time for him to stop being a victim. He needed to change. He couldn't let the world treat him this way any longer. He meditated. He thought. He pondered. He was just 17 after all; he still had time. It wasn't over. Why couldn't he have the life that he wanted? He told his family that he was going to change, that he was going to do things differently, that he realized that life didn't have to be so bad. Elliot was going to try. They were happy. He was hopeful.

Elliot thought the first thing he needed to do was to change his look. It never occurred to him that he needed to change anything inside of himself.

First he got a new haircut; one that was much more in fashion and made him look more handsome, then he bought some new clothes. He even bought jeans, something he hadn't worn for close to eight years. The clothes he bought were expensive, stylish even.

He had some hope. Maybe it was possible to have a girlfriend, have sex and have friends. Elliot even made a new Facebook profile and started to post more often in ways that he thought presented him positively.

The next time Elliot saw James, he told him about his new desire to change, to be hopeful about life. James was also a virgin who hadn't had any success with girls, but yet he had never been depressed about it either, which confused Elliot very much. How could James be a virgin and still be happy? James told Elliot that he had been worried about him, and that he was glad to hear of his newfound optimism.

It was time to think about college. This was to be a new start for Elliot. The slate was totally wiped clean; he could reinvent himself and be someone different. No one would know him. They wouldn't know he was thought of as a loser, or that he was a nerd. They wouldn't know he had been picked on. All he had to do was change his look and his vibe, and he wouldn't be lame anymore. He would be popular. Maybe girls would finally want him.

He started off slowly by attending Pierce College, a community college nearby in Woodland Hills. Many students start off at Pierce and then transfer to a more traditional university after taking some classes. He signed up for just one class. It had been a long time since he had been in any sort of normal school system, and he didn't want to overdo things. He wanted to take things slow. Elliot was a bit uptight, but optimistic. This was the start of his new life.

Around the same time, he bought his first lottery ticket. He didn't even know such things existed. He was amazed to find out that with each ticket purchased, one could become rich. This excited him greatly. He could become rich without ever having to do anything. Why had he not heard of this before?

He never had to think about money before. He had been a child. If he needed something his parents would buy it for him, and if he desired some spending money, they gave that to him. He thought to himself that if he were rich all, or at least most, of his problems would be solved. If he were rich it was obvious to him that women would want him. He had never heard of a rich man that couldn't get laid or find a girlfriend. In his mind they simply don't exist. He thought all women wanted to be with a rich man, no matter what they looked like or what their personality was. Wealthy men could be fat, ugly, or old, and they could still be with the hottest women around. The lottery could help him achieve this.

College began. Elliot still didn't have his license, so he was forced to take the bus which made him feel pathetic. Getting off the bus to attend class was not the entrance to college he craved. He felt nervous on his first day, but things seemed different. It was obvious that he wouldn't be openly picked on by anyone in college as that simply wasn't cool for anyone to do in this environment, so he felt somewhat safe. It was already better than high school, although that wasn't saying much.

Soon after college began, Soumaya came home from Morocco. She wasn't at all pleased by the way Elliot acted on his trip with her. In her opinion, he had shamed her in front of her family. It seemed that Elliot had finally crossed a line. Numerous arguments ensued, and some of them became rather intense. Elliot refused to let her push him around anymore, and she refused to continue to let Elliot be so disrespectful towards her. Before long, things came to a head and she kicked him out of the house. He began to live at his mother's house full time. He wasn't even allowed to visit his father's home.

This was just another sign to Elliot how weak his father was. As the eldest son, Elliot felt his needs should come before whatever woman was sleeping with his father. All respect Elliot had for Peter was gone forever.

Elliot continued to take walks around his mother's neighborhood, hoping that he would be approached by a random girl. He would try to look confident and appealing as he strolled around. This never happened of course. At times he would walk to a local Barnes and Noble and hang out all day reading books, hoping he might meet a girl or some friends, but he never did. Again, Elliot never approached a girl and said hello, rather he struck a pose or tried to look appealing in some way and waited for the girl to approach him.

He began to stalk people he didn't know on Facebook, reading details of their lives, ones that were always so superior to his own. This upset him and made him envious, but was also something he could use to get information. At one point, he found there was to be a huge house party not very far from his house. He decided to go. Maybe he would finally meet a girl to have sex with or at the least get some positive affirmation from the opposite sex. He still had no license, so he walked to the house, which was 45 minutes away by foot.

His heart was beating in his throat when he arrived at the party, but he forced himself to go inside. Sadly, the party was much smaller than he thought. Everyone seemed to know each other, and they were all sitting around smoking weed. He stood out like a sore thumb. He hung around awkwardly for a minute or two before escaping and heading home.

As he was walking back home in defeat, a bunch of kids in a pickup truck drove by and threw eggs at him, laughing. They missed, but he was still enraged at this indignity. He lost it and picked up one of the shells and threw it back at them, screaming at the top of his lungs. They got out of the truck and started to come towards him like they might attack him. It quickly became obvious to Elliot they were very drunk. Elliot always carried a pocketknife when he walked alone. He pulled it out and faced them down. The combination of the knife and him looking absolutely insane caused his antagonizers to back away, get in their truck, and leave.

He obsessed for days about what happened. He felt he was attacked because he looked weak. He was alone and small. He was through being messed with. His mother's apartment complex had a gym. He started to work out there just about every day. He thought if he were strong, people would leave him alone. If he were strong, girls would like him.

Over time Soumaya became less angry with Elliot, or at least chose to hide it once again, and he was invited over for dinner on occasion. Still, she disgusted Elliot, but he kept it inside. He still needed her and Peter as much as he hated to admit it. He had to pretend he liked Soumaya, smile at her, and talk to her about his life.

Peter started to teach Elliot to drive. Like most things were for Elliot, it was terrifying. He didn't feel ready to take his driver's test and drive places on his own. He still felt like a child. Driving a car is what adults do. Although it would be nice to have a car that he could use to impress girls, he hated the thought of having to drive himself places.

Life was still awful for him. Although he had attempted to change his attitude, had gone to college, and even tried to go to a party, he was having no success with his plans to have a social life or a girlfriend. He spent much of his time frustrated and filled with hate. He had done everything he could possibly do, and still the world offered him nothing. There seemed to be no place for him to turn.

One night his mother threw a small party where Elliot saw Maddy, the girl he had played with as a child, the one that he bathed with. Now she was grown, beautiful, and popular. Elliot tried to talk to her, but his overtures went nowhere. He could tell how odd he seemed to her. She was filled with life and hope, and Elliot felt he was nothing but a weirdo. Didn't she remember the wonderful times they once shared together? Or did she remember and was ashamed to let on because her social stature was so much above his now?

Elliot attempted to reconnect with two old friends, Phillip and Addison, but when they hung out, Addison kept talking about girls he had met and parties he had been to. Elliot thought this was ridiculous, Addison was just trying to be cool. Or he might even be lying. Elliot became angry because he felt Addison was treating him like a loser. He was showing him no respect.

He continued to take solace by going on long walks. Sometimes he would walk for hours, hoping that he would meet a girl who found him attractive. Or even one who found him interesting. It never happened. Elliot could not figure out what he was doing wrong.

College was a disaster. Elliot still felt like a fool taking the bus; in his mind he might as well be wearing a clown outfit to class. He made no friends, and felt people didn't even notice him. Of course, Elliot never approached anyone else either.

He soon gave up and dropped the one class he was taking. What was the point if he wasn't going to have sex? This made his mother very upset, so much so that she wanted Elliot to actually get a job and threatened to kick him out until he got one. He couldn't believe it. Now his mother wanted him to get a job? Could things get any worse?

He did a bit of searching for a job online, but he couldn't find one that he wanted. All the jobs he was qualified for he thought were for losers. He wasn't going to do some awful job that he felt was beneath him. He worried that things were just going to get worse. The older he got the more was expected of him. He was going to have to work at some ridiculous hourly job like some sort of peasant? And then go home to some crappy apartment by himself? And do what? Watch TV? Play *World of Warcraft?* He would rather die.

Since he wasn't going to college and had a lot of spare time, he decided to educate himself. Every day he walked to Barnes and Noble to read books about powerful world leaders and philosophers as well as self-help and psychology books. He continued to search for the key that would open up the world he so desired.

While his mind was full, his heart remained empty. He would see couples there, hanging out, doing what couples do. Elliot wrote: "Sometimes they would even sit on the reading chairs, kissing and fondling each other. Whenever I saw this, I got so overcome by envy and heartbreak that I went to the bathroom to cry. "

Since he had nothing else to do, sometimes he would still hang out with Addison, but he began to despise him more every day. Addison told Elliot of all the fun he was having in his life and how many girls he hung out with, and Elliot felt rage. He even accused Addison of lying and making up how popular he was just to make Elliot feel bad, which just made Addison laugh. Finally Addison even deleted Elliot from his list of Facebook friends. This was just too much. Elliot sent him a message filled with seething anger telling Addison just what he thought of him. Addison ignored it.

Life was not fair. Once Elliot and Addison were on a similar path, then for reasons Elliot couldn't fathom, Addison became more popular than he was. Because of this, Addison placed himself at a higher station in life, and he decided to treat Elliot badly. Purely because he could. This was just another example to Elliot about how life was nothing but a battle where only the strongest survive. And to Elliot's despair, he believed that he was weak.

Elliot continued to expand on his personal philosophy that those having the most sex should be punished and that sex was evil. As Elliot wrote:

> My hope that I will one day have a beautiful girlfriend and live the life I desire slowly faded away. I was in the same dark and miserable place I had been a year previously; lonely, unwanted, miserable, and seething with rage at the world. I kept thinking about how some boys were easily able to get girlfriends straight after they went through puberty. I couldn't fathom how they did it, and I hated and despised them for it.

It seemed to him he had no choice anymore. He decided to fight against the world, the one that had hurt him so much, that had destroyed his hopes and dreams. It was either battle back or accept the fate the cruel world had pushed upon him. And Elliot did not think of himself as a quitter.

He wasn't going to be able to do that unemployed though apparently. His mother kept pressuring him to get a job, and the two were starting to argue. Elliot wasn't doing much to rectify this situation. He wasn't qualified for any jobs that he considered worthy of his intellect, and he refused to do jobs he could get. He could have gotten a job in retail for example, but he found the thought ridiculous. As he wrote: "I am an intellectual who is destined for greatness. I would never perform a low-class service job."

Finally his mother found him a life coach, a guy named Tony. Elliot was fine with this. At this point, his pride was so battered it barely even phased him. He had no one to hang out with anyway, so going out to lunch a few times a week with an enthusiastic 40- year-old guy who tried to teach him how to socialize and get a job wasn't the worst thing in the world.

Peter had a friend who was doing some carpentry work at his house. At Peter's request, the friend hired Elliot to help him for a few weeks. Although Elliot still thought this type of job was far beneath him, he took it to get his mother off his back. He also could pretend it wasn't even a real job. He was just helping out a buddy for a few weeks, being a nice guy.

Elliot rode his bike to work every day; it took him one-half an hour each way. The work was hard; the bike ride was challenging, and he found himself feeling better about himself for a short time. The physical exertion of each day was helping calm his mind, and even though the work was nothing he wanted to continue to do, it kept him busy at a time when he very much needed it. But then the job ended.

His first day after finishing the job, Elliot went for a bike ride. He was thirsty as he rode, so he stopped at his father's home to get a drink of water. He entered the home without knocking as he always did. He surprised Soumaya when he entered, and she got rather angry about it. She told Elliot to go back outside and knock. Elliot refused, feeling that he had rights to the home as the eldest son and got himself the glass of water that he came for. As he did so Soumaya knocked it out his hand, and it broke on the floor with a crash. Peter then entered the kitchen and took Soumaya's side. They both kicked him out of the house and told him never to come back. Elliot simply could not believe it. In his mind this was just another example of the indignities he had to face every day.

Shortly after that, Elliot had another conversation with Addison in which he hurled insults at him to get back at him for all the pain that he felt he had caused him. Addison was nonplussed and told Elliot in a rather calm way, "No girl in this whole world will ever want to fuck you."

Elliot hated all of them. They were dead to him. He felt his mother was all he had in the world.

But even his mother upset him. She had begun dating a man that was quite rich, which excited Elliot very much. He began to ask her to marry her new boyfriend. This could be a way out. If Elliot were rich, he thought everything would be okay. His mother would marry this rich man, then would give him all sorts of money, and once he was wealthy, women would flock to him. But when he brought this up to his mother, she just became irritated for reasons he couldn't understand.

Elliot finally got his driver's license. His mother gave him her old car to use pretty much whenever he wished. Now Elliot could go anywhere he wanted, when he pleased, and for the first time started to think of himself as an adult. He decided to go back to college, now that he didn't have to take the bus, it would be more tenable.

Elliot took a summer class at a community college in the Moorpark area. He liked it way better than Pierce. The campus was gorgeous and the girls were way prettier. He finally felt hope in his life again. He hoped he would meet a pretty girl at Moorpark College, and she would fall in love with him. If he had a gorgeous girl with a hot body that wanted to be his, he could stop hating the world, hating everyone. To Elliot it was pretty much as simple as that.

This feeling didn't last long. He soon saw couples walking together in areas where he walked alone. This filled him with anger. There was one particular guy in one of his classes who was taking the class with his girlfriend. As Elliot wrote: "Every day I had to see this, and my envy grew and grew. I constantly glared at them with raw hatred. What did I do wrong that he did right? I yelled out to the universe on the way home. Why does he deserve the love of a beautiful girl, and not me? Why do girls hate me so? Questions and questions. All I could do was question why I was suffering so much injustice in life."

His mother said that he should become a writer because he was good at that, or at least she thought so. Elliot decided

The "Supreme Gentleman" Killer | 89

this is how he could become rich, how he could impress everyone. He still felt he was a genius; he was meant to be famous. Why hadn't he thought of becoming a rich and successful writer before? Now all he had to do was write something, publish it, and make millions.

He started focusing on writing a story about someone rising to power in life after being treated poorly. He believed this would not only make him wealthy, but might inspire others and change society in some way.

Maybe it would be a made into a movie or at the very least become a bestselling novel. Instead of working on his college assignments, he concentrated on his writing. He already hated college; his initial optimism was gone. Many days he cried in his car on the way home because of seeing all the happy couples there.

He soon realized that there wasn't much chance of a book being made into a movie and that most writers made next to nothing. It seemed even successful ones didn't make a lot of money until they were 40 or so. He didn't want to wait that long to get laid. What would be the point? He quit writing.

He also dropped his class. He couldn't stand looking at that couple every single day. To Elliot it was almost like they took the class together just to torment him. They made him so angry.

He knew his mother would be upset that he blew off his class, so he called his life coach Tony about getting a job. He felt if he found some employment at least he could tell his mother he dropped his class without her blowing up.

Tony said he knew of someone who was hiring, and Elliot accepted the job on the spot. When he showed up for work, he found out it was basically a janitor job in an office building. Elliot worked part of one day then quit. He was perplexed. What was Tony thinking? A man with his intellect could never be a janitor. It was ridiculous to even think about. This was the only real job he ever had. It lasted a few hours.

Elliot told his mother he would take more classes at Moorpark, and he would keep working hard on his writing. She understood, or maybe she was just tired of it all, or it could be she understood how much her son was struggling. Either way, she didn't mess with him too much.

Elliot spent the summer miserable as always. Alone, thinking about how everyone had it better than he did. He was 19 and still a virgin. It was almost too much for him to bear.

On his 19th birthday his father didn't call. Instead, he sent a letter asking Elliot to apologize to Soumaya. Elliot ignored it.

Elliot hadn't played *World of Warcraft* for well over a year, but that summer he started again. What else was he to do? As soon as he logged on to his main toon, he got a message from James.

He was back. He started to go over to James's house to play *WoW* on occasion. James was also a virgin, which made Elliot happy, although he was confused as to why James wasn't incredibly angry about it. Elliot looked at his anger about his lot in life as a sign of great strength. He wasn't just going to sit there and take what everyone was doing to him. He knew even then that one day he would have his revenge.

He spent the summer playing *WoW* and reading the book series *A Song of Ice and Fire,* by George R.R. Martin, the same series that was eventually made into *Game of Thrones.* Elliot loved it.

Elliot took another class at Moorpark College, in part to keep his mother off his back and in part so he could tell himself he was doing something. Anything. It went poorly. The teacher sometimes called on him to answer questions in the class, which terrified him. He continued to be upset when he saw couples walking in the halls. He still cried when he drove home each day.

Out of boredom ,Elliot started to take drives at night around his neighborhood. He soon stopped doing so on weekends as he would often see groups of teenagers together hanging out.

A new expansion, "Cataclysm," came out on *WoW*. Elliot bought it and spent two weeks straight playing it pretty much every waking hour, until once again he decided again to quit. He felt the creators of the game had made changes that weren't for the best; the game was now too easy; it was "nerfed" if you will. But the main reason was that all of a sudden a lot of normal people were playing the game. *WoW* kept getting more popular, and because of that the game was ruined for him.

People now spent time in game chat writing about having sex with girls. People used the word "virgin" as a way to insult others. If one was really good at the game, a popular insult used by the normals was to say that players like Elliot had no lives. Since Elliot was a virgin and felt he had no life and this made him angry. *WoW* used to be a place where he went to get away from these types of people. Now he had no safe place left.

Elliot told James that he was going to quit *WoW* again. James wasn't surprised, and he mentioned to Elliot how he had noticed how angry he seemed about a lot of the new players. Elliot questioned James about why he wasn't angry as well? After all he was a 19-year-old virgin just like Elliot. James said he just focused on his strengths and didn't care about things like that. Elliot found this ridiculous. James said he was focusing on his strengths, but in reality Elliot felt he was incredibly weak.

Soon New Year's Eve came, Elliot was alone as he was every year. He got on his *WoW* account and started messing with people and insulting those who seemed "normal," but they just laughed him off.

He decided once more that this year things would be different, he would make changes, and things would be better. He made a New Year's resolution that he wouldn't masturbate until he did at least one new thing that was a positive in his life. He made it seven days before he broke down. When he touched himself he thought of the same thing he always did—having normal sex with a tall blonde girl. As odd as Elliot Rodger was, his fantasies were always vanilla.

Elliot's mother and father took him for dinner at a Japanese restaurant; they wanted to have a talk with him about life and about his future. They told him that they thought he needed to move out, that staying at home was just allowing him to wallow in his misery. He needed some stimulation in his life, some direction. He was a young man. He needed something to do.

It was at this very moment Elliot decided he would move to Santa Barbara, although he had been thinking of this for quite some time now. Years ago he had watched a movie called *Alpha Dog*. The movie was filled with all sorts of attractive young people hanging out, partying, and having sex. It was filmed in Santa Barbara. If he had never seen *Alpha Dog*, who knows where his trajectory would have taken him. Who knows where his Day of Retribution would have occurred or if it would have happened at all.

Elliot had read about a town called Isla Vista, which was right next to the University of California, Santa Barbara, as well as Santa Barbara City College where Elliot would eventually take classes. It was known as a playground for college kids, where they all lived, partied, and got laid. Maybe if he moved there, he would have this life too.

If one looks up the town of Isla Vista, one of the first things found is this definition from Urban Dictionary:

> *An almost too-good-to-be-true college student playground nestled in fabulous Santa Barbara where the apartments are absolute shit yet $650/mo to share a room. At night, IV crawls with thousands of piss-drunk students, all walking from house to house sucking up the greater half of California's*

vodka supply. Sadly, nearly half of these party-goers are arrested by the Isla Vista foot patrol for DIPs (Drunk in Publics). Isla Vista is an overall awesome place to spend your college years.

This is what Elliot wanted. This would be his Nirvana.

His parents were all for the idea. His father would pay his tuition and give him $500 a month to spend on whatever he wanted. His mother would pay for his apartment and give him a car to use.

Elliot was taken aback. It all happened so fast. But maybe that was a good thing? He would be starting anew where no one knew him. He would have his own place, his own car; he could start fresh. Be someone different. Yes, he would have to share an apartment with other students, but that could be good too, he would find it easier to meet more people that way.

His father gave him a book called *The Secret*. Elliot was enthralled. It was a bestselling self-help book about the Law of Attraction. The premise of the book was that his thoughts could change his life directly. If he had negative thoughts, bad things will happen; if he thought positively, good things will happen. In this theory, both people as well as their thoughts are pure energy. In essence, what he believed would happen, would happen. Elliot thought maybe he could simply change his life just by visualizing what he wanted to happen. Could it be that simple?

He drove to the cliffs in Malibu and looked out at the powerful, endless ocean and told the infinite universe that he wanted to be rich. He proclaimed that he wanted gorgeous and sexy woman to desire him and he wanted everyone that had ever looked down on him to envy him.

Once done with these proclamations, he walked the beach. It wasn't long before he crossed paths with a man holding hands with a woman who Elliot considered to be incredibly hot. Although Elliot felt some anger at this man, who he assumed to be rich, he also felt hope. This man was in his early thirties, so Elliot thought he still had time to become rich and have what he had. It wouldn't be long now.

He went to a convenience store on the way home and bought a lottery ticket and visualized himself winning. He held great hope that he would win. He lost of course. It angered him greatly that he believed, even for a moment, in that stupid book and how it said life could be better.

He started to take karate classes with James for something to do. For a while he enjoyed it. He got to see James every week, and he was working on being stronger and more impressive, so he could impress women and possibly become a true Alpha. But the class had started to irritate him as of late. For one thing, there was a younger kid in the class who looked down on Elliot because he had a brown belt while Elliot had only a white belt. For another thing, James was not only quite a bit stronger than Elliot, he was a lot better at karate than he was too. It was just one more thing Elliot wasn't very good at. At times Elliot showed his anger while he was fighting, which to him felt good, but the teachers frowned on it.

After class James and Elliot usually went to get a bite to eat. When they did Elliot would often see young couples out enjoying themselves. This pissed off Elliot to no end. He told James how angry he was when he saw people rubbing their happiness in his face all the time. He shared with him his fantasies of revenge and how he would torture those that had been mean to him if he ever came to power. They would all be sorry for how they treated him. James told Elliot to stop, that it was too much, he couldn't take it anymore. Elliot didn't understand why James was so upset; he was one of the few people he wouldn't torture after all.

Elliot decided to quit the karate class. He didn't see James again until months later.

He also stopped going to classes at Moorpark College. He didn't drop the class; he just didn't show up anymore.

He kept that bit of information to himself though. He told his mother school was great and everything was fine, but when he was supposed to be at class, he hung out at a Barnes and Noble until his mother left for work then he came back home. She had no idea he was lying. He was very good at that. The last day of class he showed up, took his finals, got in his car, drove home, and cried alone in his room.

The only thing that kept him going was that he knew beyond a shadow of a doubt he was destined for great things. Maybe he would find them in Santa Barbara. Everything that happened in his life up to now was just a test of some sort.

His mother told Elliot that he had to move to Santa Barbara in early June, well before school started in the fall. In Elliot's mind he knew that she was just sick of dealing with him, so much so she was willing to pay rent to have him gone. Even his mother was tired of him now.

Elliot went to Isla Vista with his mother and father to look at some potential apartments. When Elliot saw Isla Vista for the first time, he was amazed. It was everything he had imagined; a town filled with college students all living together and partying together. This could be paradise. Hot blondes were everywhere he looked.

Elliot always felt part of the reason he was troubled was that he lived with his mother in her apartment. He wasn't projecting the right image to the women of the world. No gorgeous blonde wanted to go out with someone who lived with his mother. This would be different. How could he *not* get laid here? It would be virtually impossible.

It was decided that, even though Elliot would be sharing an apartment with other students, he needed his own room. A shared bedroom was simply out of the question to Elliot. They chose a place called Capri Apartments. He was to live in a two-bedroom apartment and have his own room, while two other students shared the other bedroom. He would be moving in on June 4. Elliot spent his remaining time at his mother's home working out to make his body look better and shopping for clothes. This was his big opportunity for change, and he didn't want to blow it.

For once Elliot had some hope. He believed Santa Barbara was his last chance, or to him rather, it was the world's last chance to make things right.

As he wrote:

> *I am an intelligent gentleman, and I deserve the love of girls more than the other obnoxious boys of my age, and yet they get girls and I don't. That is a crime that can never be forgotten, nor can it be forgiven. I always wanted to exact my revenge on humanity for forcing me to live such a life, but I've also always had the hope that if I can do things in life to make up for all my suffering, then that in itself would be a form of peaceful revenge. In truth, the move to Santa Barbara was actually a chance that I was giving to the world, not the other way around! I was giving the world one last chance to give me the life that I know I'm entitled to, the life that other boys are able to live with ease. If I still have to suffer the same rejection and injustice even after I move to Santa Barbara, then that will be the last straw. I will have my vengeance.*

THE LAW OF ATTRACTION

On June 4, 2011, Elliot Rodger said goodbye to his mother and drove off to Santa Barbara to be on his own for the first time. It was a bittersweet moment. Elliot would miss his mother, but he knew it was time for him to become a man.

His father met him at his new apartment to help him move in. He soon met his two temporary housemates; they were only going to be there for a week. One of them was tall and blonde. This annoyed Elliot to no end, but he kept his feelings inside; he didn't want to get off on the wrong foot, and besides he would be gone soon.

After a quick lunch at a local restaurant, his father left. For the first time in his life, Elliot was alone. He was frightened, terrified really, but he also had some hope. This was a big opportunity; one he had never experienced before. He talked a bit to his roommates, and they seemed okay. They weren't overtly mean to him or anything and seemed easy enough to get along with.

His first night did not go well. As he lay in his bed he heard students outside, partying, yelling, having a good time. This scared him. He didn't feel ready. His heart thumped in his chest as he lay in bed.

Would he ever be able to just be that person outside having fun, or would he always be hiding in his bed alone, terrified? Then, later that evening he heard two people loudly having sex in the apartment above him. The woman screamed when she orgasmed. This enraged him. Now he didn't just have to know that people other than him were having sex, but he actually had to listen to it as well?

His two roommates were nice enough, but they kept inviting over a friend named Chance, who happened to be black, to hang out. Elliot hated how cocky he was. Elliot felt Chance walked around like he was something special, like he was better than Elliot.

One day Chance started talking about how well he did with girls. For some reason, Elliot decided to ask the three of them if they were virgins. He knew it was a mistake, but he couldn't help it. They all looked at Elliot like he was something very peculiar, then told him that they all had lost their virginity a long time ago. Chance said he lost his when he was just 13 years old. To a blonde white girl no less. Elliot told him that he was a liar, then went to his room and cried.

As he wrote:

> *How could an inferior, ugly black boy be able to get a white girl and not me? I am beautiful, and I am half white myself. I am descended from British aristocracy. He is descended from slaves. I deserve it more. I tried not to believe his foul words, but they were already said, and it was hard to erase from my mind. If this is actually true, if this ugly black filth was able to have sex with a blonde white girl at the age of thirteen while I've had to suffer virginity all my life, then this just proves how ridiculous the female gender is. They would give themselves to this filthy scum, but they reject ME? The injustice!*

In Isla Vista, Elliot became even more convinced that females had inferior minds, and they were inherently flawed. He continued to see a bevy of super-hot young woman walking around with who he felt were stupid jocks, and not "intelligent gentlemen" like he was. This false realization that there was something purely wrong with women's brains made Elliot feel worse than ever. It wasn't like he could do something himself to change things because no matter what he did, women were still going to be stupid fools.

His two temporary housemates left, and two more moved in who would be there for the rest of the month. One was Daniel and the other was Reed. Daniel was very nice and made it a point to talk to Elliot, which he enjoyed. Reed was a quiet Asian-American who was studying biology.

Elliot took two classes over the summer, one of which started at eight in the morning. On the day of his first class, his alarm went off, and he hopped out of bed, ready to take on the day. He put on a new shirt, which Elliot considered quite fashionable, jumped in his car, and headed off to class. It was a fresh start.

For once Elliot felt confident as he headed to class at Santa Barbara City College. As he walked past girls, he imagined they were attracted to him, that they liked his shirt, that they were intrigued by him. They had to be wondering who he was, where he was from, what his background was. He was an interesting and attractive young man, starting his first day of school.

There were some pretty young women hanging around outside of the building where his first class was. Elliot fixed a very confident look on his face and tried to make eye contact with them as he walked by, but they didn't even seem to notice him. This bothered him a bit, but he wasn't going to let anything affect his confidence today.

As Elliot entered his classroom, he took his time and picked out a seat that he wanted, but as soon as he sat down, a group of guys, who obviously were the popular type, sat down next to him. He thought they were obvious and lame, and yet they seemed to know all the different pretty girls in the class. These were the type of guys Elliot had despised all his life. Elliot hated them. He didn't think he could compete with them, and in his mind they would never accept him as one of them.

He wouldn't give up though. He believed this was his last chance to have the life he wanted for himself. He walked around campus and saw tons of pretty girls just hanging out everywhere he looked. He wanted to go up and ask one of them out, but he couldn't summon up the courage. He worried they might think he was weird.

At the end of his first day, he took a drive around Santa Barbara only to see numerous happy couples walking together, holding hands, smiling at each other. Elliot suddenly realized that things might be even worse here than anywhere else. If he couldn't succeed with women here, when they're literally anywhere, where could he succeed? Elliot felt the fear rise inside of him again. He hadn't thought of this aspect of things.

He dropped that class almost immediately. It was too much for him to deal with, seeing all of those "bros" chat up all those pretty girls day after day while not paying any attention to Elliot at all. It wasn't worth the torture.

One day he got one of his roomies to buy him some vodka. Elliot wasn't much of a drinker. He had never gone to any parties or hung out with anyone who drank, but he started a routine on the weekend of taking a shot or two and going out to walk around by himself, in the midst of thousands of partying people his age, hoping he would meet pretty girls, or at least friends. He never did. Of course he never approached any of them either.

One night he was drunk enough to actually go up to a bunch of other students that were hanging out in a common area of his apartment complex. It started off okay, but then Elliot just sat there in silence, not sure what to say. One of the other students asked him why he was so quiet. Which of course made things worse. The one thing someone should never do when around a person who isn't saying much is ask why they are so quiet. They gave him a few beers though, which Elliot sat and drank with them, still not knowing what to say. Later he stumbled back to his room and vomited on the floor before he passed out in his bed. This was one of the most social things that Elliot had done in years. Maybe ever.

Elliot went home for a few days around the Fourth of July where he saw James at a holiday party and hung out with his parents a bit. They all seemed proud of him for going off to school on his own. Although in Elliot's mind things were not going well at all in his life, it was still nice to know others thought he was doing well.

When he returned to school a few days later, it was time to move into his permanent apartment. He said goodbye to his roomies. Although he wasn't close to them, they actually weren't that bad, and it gave Elliot hope that his next situation might be even better. His new roommates wouldn't be moving in until August, which meant Elliot had the rest of July with the place all to himself. He was happy about this, but was nervous about who his new roommates were to be.

His father came to visit him and took him out to dinner, but it didn't go very well. As Elliot relates:

> *When we sat down at our table, I saw a young couple sitting a few tables down the row. The sight of them enraged me to no end, especially because it was a dark-skinned Mexican guy dating a hot blonde white girl. I regarded it as a great insult to my dignity. How could an inferior Mexican guy be able to date a white blonde girl, while I was still suffering as a lonely virgin? I was ashamed to be in such an inferior position in front my father. When I saw the two of them kissing, I could barely contain my rage. I stood up in anger, and I was about to walk up to them and pour my glass of soda all over their heads. I probably would have, if father wasn't there. I was seething with envious rage, and my father was there to watch it all. It was so humiliating. I wasn't the son I wanted to present*

to my father. I should be the one with the hot blonde girl, making my father proud. Instead, my father had to watch me suffer in a pathetic position. Life is so cruel to me. When I said my farewell to father before he drove home, I felt absolutely miserable. I then went back to my room and sulked for hours.

The next day it got even worse. Elliot went to get a coffee at Starbucks when he saw a guy making out with a girl in line. Elliot lost it. Why were they doing this to him? When they left Starbucks he followed them to their car and splashed his coffee all over them. The boy yelled at Elliot, and he quickly ran away. When he got in his car, he was shaking with excitement. He had struck back! Yes, it didn't accomplish much, but it was still a form of vengeance. Yet he knew he still lost, even after splashing them with coffee. That guy got to go home with this hot, young woman, while he went home alone.

He wished he had power over that couple. He wanted to kill them. He had these type of thoughts numerous times in the past, but this was different. For the first time, he felt capable of doing so. If he had the chance to kill his enemies, he would. He wanted to torture them, kill them slowly. Rip their skin from their bones.

Elliot spent the next five days in his room. Every time he looked out his window he saw young people outside hanging out together, having fun, laughing, while he sat in his bed alone, miserable, and terrified. He began to fantasize about entering people's rooms while they're having sex and slaughtering them with a knife.

One day Elliot realized he only had 12 days before he turned 20, and he was still a virgin. He felt had to do something. If he turned 20 without ever having sex, he felt it would be a catastrophe. He would feel like such a fool.

He spent most of those days sitting outside at a table in front of the Isla Vista Domino's Pizza, waiting for a girl to come up and talk to him, hoping the conversation would lead to sex. Obviously, it didn't work. Once he walked past a woman that he thought was pretty, and he worked up the courage to look at her and say hello, but she didn't even respond to him. She even looked away. He went into a stall in a public bathroom and cried for an hour.

One day, a few days before he stopped being a teenager, he went for an aimless drive. He saw a beautiful girl and a good-looking jock kissing each other in public, showing off their lust for the world to see. He simply couldn't believe it. The couple stopped making out and started to walk down the road. Elliot followed them in his car for a bit, then opened his window, splashed his iced tea all over them and drove away as quickly as he could.

Things weren't changing, he wasn't having sex or gaining power: they were just getting worse. To his great dismay, Elliot turned 20 and was still a virgin. The unthinkable had happened. Not only that, no one seemed to realize how incredibly awful and humiliating it was for him.

For this 20th birthday his parents took him to a fancy restaurant in Encino with his sister. They all seemed to not have any idea how miserable Elliot was and acted like everything was fine in Elliot's life and that his birthday was some sort of happy event instead of one of the worst days of his life. This made Elliot very angry.

Elliot spent his time on summer vacation buying new clothes to make himself feel better and hanging out alone, except for occasionally spending time with James. It was an uneventful time for Elliot, one filled with misery, although he still had rare moments of hope. If there was one thing Elliot Rodger was not, it was a quitter. He still thought he would not only survive this, but he would come out on top.

When he went back to college in August, two more roomies, Ryan and Angel, awaited him. Elliot was extremely disappointed to find out that they were Hispanic, which meant to him they were from a much lower social class. Not only that, they already knew each other, which worried him because in his mind they could gang up on Elliot if they chose to do so. Elliot couldn't believe his bad luck.

On the very second day in the apartment, they invited some friends over to hang out. The friends also seemed low class to Elliot. He didn't fit in at all. Everyone started talking and before long Elliot was asked if he was a virgin. He was stunned. There he was, minding his own business in his own apartment, and he was asked about his greatest shame in front of a group of people?

He said that he was, he never lied about such things. Then Ryan and Angel and some of the others began to tell Elliot about all the girls they had sex with over the years. Elliot was enraged. Angel was not only Hispanic, but Elliot thought he was ugly, while he thought of himself as beautiful. How could this happen that women would have sex with Angel and not him?

He was so mad he went to his bedroom. He punched the wall in anger. When he did, he could hear them all laughing at him.

The next day Elliot and Angel almost fought. As he wrote:

> *The ugly pig kept acting as if girls thought he was more attractive than me. Hah! I am a beautiful, magnificent gentleman and he is a low-class, pig-faced thug. I had enough of his cocksure attitude, and I started to call him exactly what he was. I tried to insult him as much as I could, telling him how superior I am to him, and saying that he was low-class. He tried to attack me, but Ryan, being the more mellow of the two, held him back. A pity, I was itching for a chance to hurt that obnoxious little animal.*

Elliot called his mother and told her what was happening and that he couldn't live with these vile creatures. His mother, almost certainly didn't agree with his assessment of his roommates, but she did want to protect her son, so she and Elliot soon arranged for him to be transferred to a room that only had one roommate, which he liked much better although it was more expensive. At least he wouldn't be ganged up on anymore.

He had to stay for the rest of the month during which Angel and Ryan kept telling him how often they were going to be getting laid and making fun of Elliot for being a virgin. Elliot wanted to murder them both, and felt more than capable of doing so, but he knew the time was not right. He had so much more planning to do. He didn't want to waste his freedom on killing what he considered to be two, low-class Hispanics. What kind of statement would that be? That would change nothing in the world.

During the weekends, he usually went home and stayed with his mother, and while home at times he hung out with James. One day he and James drove to Topanga Canyon and went to eat at a Chinese restaurant they both had been to before. Almost as soon as they sat down, a bunch of high school kids walked in, jocks and their pretty girlfriends.

James immediately said, "We're fucked" under his breath. He knew Elliot was going to freak out. After all, he had been through such things before. This wasn't his first rodeo when it came to Elliot and how he acted around good-looking couples. Elliot became so upset he wanted to pour his drink over one boy's head, but James persuaded him to leave. As they drove, Elliot told James each act of revenge he wanted to enact on each of those popular kids. He wanted to flay them alive. He wanted to hear them scream.

It was obvious to Elliot that his fantasies were disturbing James, which disgusted him even more. He wanted to take back power from those he considered animals that were in the social ruling class, but James didn't have his back. He began to think James was weak. Elliot might appear to be nothing now, but in time that would change. But the longer the two talked, the more Elliot's toughness vanished, until he cried in front of James and told him how much he hated life, how overwhelmed he was. James was kind, but, it was obvious to them both, a line had been crossed. That was pretty much the end of that friendship, the only one that Elliot had.

When back at school, he continued to walk the streets of Isla Vista hoping to find a girl he could take home with him, to prove to his roomies that girls liked him too. As always he would never talk to these women. He would just dress the way he thought he should, fix a cocky expression on his face, and stand somewhere, or walk somewhere, waiting for women to approach him and tell him how attracted they were to him.

But they didn't. Never. Not ever. One night he saw a boy walking with TWO pretty girls. He blew up. He followed them for a few minutes cursing at them and hurling insults, but they just laughed at him. He ran home crying.

Fall semester began. Elliot had three classes this semester, which kept him at school for the entire day. All day he roamed the halls or sat in the library, looking at beautiful girls, hoping to meet one. None wanted him, or even noticed him for that matter. He didn't meet any friends either. If he met friends, then he might be invited to parties, and maybe he could meet girls that way.

At least Elliot was able to move into his new apartment. He was finally away from his roomies that he hated so much. He had his new place to himself for a bit before his new roommate moved in. When he set up his room, he looked at his new bedroom and thought to himself , "Maybe this is finally the place I will lose my virginity."

So far Santa Barbara was a complete failure. This was supposed to be a time of Elliot's life where things were going to change; he was supposed to become popular, find a girlfriend, have sex, at least once, but none of it happened. All day long he watched happy couples hanging out and hooking up while he seethed inside.

He got so lonely that he even started playing *WoW* again for a time, but it had lost its magic. James still played, and Elliot tried to engage him when he saw him online, but James seemed to have no interest in really talking to Elliot. When Elliot called James out on it, sending him private messages asking why he was being ignored, James stopped responding to Elliot at all.

His new roommate arrived. Spencer was a bit older than Elliot, friendly, and not intimidating at all. This was okay, but he was also chubby, and definitely not someone Elliot would ever be friends with, or who could help Elliot achieve his social goals. Not only that, but apparently Spencer used to have a girlfriend. It was ridiculous to Elliot that someone fat and unattractive was able to meet a girl. Spencer was even shorter than Elliot. The whole thing was absurd to him. The only thing that made Elliot feel better was imagining that Spencer's girlfriend must have been short and fat herself. It was the only thing that made sense to Elliot.

While Spencer wasn't totally irritating, he still bothered Elliot immensely for one main reason. Spencer bore witness to how pathetic Elliot felt his life was, and Elliot couldn't stand that. In the entire world, Spencer was the only person who knew that Elliot had no life at all. That despite how amazing he thought he looked, and despite the fact he was a gentleman, he still had not one single girl's phone number in his phone contacts.

He worried he would be a virgin forever. That, even at such a place at Santa Barbara City College, after one entire semester, he never even got close to getting laid. He might be able to fool the rest of the world, but he could never fool Spencer, and this angered him.

He spent the Christmas break at home doing nothing and hanging out by himself. He spent some time shopping, spending his mother's money, buying designer clothes such as Armani suits.

He decided to try to appear more sophisticated, more European. He even affected a bit of an accent. He didn't want to be a bro, a jock, or a dude. He wanted to be a gentleman.

Shortly after he arrived back in Santa Barbara things took a turn for the worse with his roommate Spencer. Up until then, the two had gotten along fine. Although they hadn't really spent any time together, they weren't openly hostile to each other either, which for Elliot was a definite boon.

But then one morning, when Elliot woke up, he realized to his horror, Spencer had a girl in his room. Elliot was shocked. This short and tubby person was able to get laid and he wasn't? It wasn't that Elliot thought she was attractive, of course she wasn't, that would have been silly, but still Spencer having a girl in his room was almost beyond the pale. Even worse, when he saw Spencer, he gave Elliot a bit of a smug look about it, acting like he was better than him. Later that night when the girl was gone, Elliot talked to Spencer, telling him that he was a fool because he was proud to have had sex with an ugly whore. He told Spencer that anyone could do something like that; Elliot certainly could; he just chose not to debase himself in such a manner, while Spencer would basically screw any fat pig that would have him. This made Spencer angry, which was what Elliot wanted. Things weren't the same after that.

On the first day of his spring semester, Elliot put on his favorite Armani shirt and a pair of Gucci sunglasses. He had stepped up his fashion game hard, and his hair was perfect. He looked at himself in the mirror for a bit and liked what he saw. He posed a little and winked at himself. He knew today some girl would want him. As he wrote he "set off for my college with the confidence that I would appear as a superior gentleman to all of the students there. I *was* a superior gentleman. That was what I was born to be, and it was now time to show it to the world."

When he got to school, he went to the restroom and looked at himself. He looked perfect. He said to his reflection, "I am the image of beauty and supremacy." He said it over and over again. As he walked to class he looked at everyone he saw and told himself that every guy admired him and every woman wanted him. He purposely waited for his first class to start before going in, so he would be noticed. He couldn't wait to see all the heads turn and look at him. But when he walked in, no one seemed to care. He was a bit taken aback, but thought it was possible people might be too intimidated by him.

The next day Elliot was taking an aimless drive when he saw two pretty blondes standing by the side of the road talking to each other. Elliot was wearing one of his expensive shirts. He was driving a nice car and he was, of course, the image of beauty and supremacy. He was certain of this.

He slowed down the car and smiled at them as he drove past. They looked disgusted then quickly looked away. Elliot was enraged. He drove down the road for a bit, turned around, pulled up in front of them and splashed his Starbucks latte all over their perfect bodies then drove away as fast as he could. Their screams were music to his ears. He just wished that his latte was hotter. He wanted to burn them. He wished he could throw them in a vat of boiling water and watch their skin melt off as they screamed.

He became obsessed with a girl in his math class. She was blonde, beautiful, just perfect. He thought of her constantly and pleasured himself to thoughts of her at night. In his fantasies he made love to her like a gentleman, slowly while looking deeply into her eyes.

Of course she didn't notice him at all. No matter how often he looked at her, what clothes he wore, how perfect his hair was; she never deigned to even look at him. Elliot was perplexed.

He looked her up on Facebook and found that she not only had a boyfriend, but he was someone Elliot thought was a stupid looking jock. The kind of person that made Elliot mad just by looking at him. He fantasized about kidnapping them both and flaying the skin off the boyfriend while he tied her up and forced her to watch. He sat in his room and screamed and cried with pain. He didn't even care that Spencer heard him.

It was all too much. He couldn't take that class anymore and dropped it. How could he sit there and look at her each day with desire knowing that some total asshole was constantly banging her? Then, once he did that, he dropped all of his other classes too. Why go? Girls didn't like him. To Elliot there was no point in having any sort of academic or professional success if he was going to continue to be so miserable.

He lost all hope. He would be a virgin forever. He would he humiliated forever. He thought to himself women were attracted to the wrong kind of person because something was wrong with their minds. They were weak and stupid. They shouldn't even be allowed to choose who they have sex with.

Sadly he came to believe all that was left was revenge. He felt he had no other choice really. He had thought about it for years. How lovely it would be to kill and torture happy couples, but it was just a fantasy. This was in part because Elliot still had some hope that he might someday have a happy life. Those days were gone. He believed there was nothing else.

As Elliot wrote:

> *It was only when I first moved to Santa Barbara that I started considering the possibility of having to carry out a violent act of revenge, as the final solution to dealing with all of the injustices I've had to face at the hands of women and society. I came up with a name for this after I saw all of the good looking young couples walking around my college and in the town of Isla Vista. I named it the Day of Retribution. It would be a day in which I exact*

my ultimate retribution and revenge on all of the hedonistic scum who enjoyed lives of pleasure that they don't deserve. If I can't have it, I will destroy it. I will destroy all women because I can never have them. I will make them all suffer for rejecting me. I will arm myself with deadly weapons and wage a war against all women and the men they are attracted to. And I will slaughter them like the animals they are. If they won't accept me among them, then they are my enemies. They showed me no mercy, and in turn I will show them no mercy. The prospect will be so sweet, and justice will ultimately be served. And of course, I would have to die in the act to avoid going to prison.

For the first time, he began to think that his Day of Retribution was not only possible, but perhaps something he really could do. Not only something that he could do, but that he should do. Someone had to do something drastic to change how awful the world had become. Why not him? He believed this had all been going on for way too long, and it needed to stop.

He wrote about his plans once, but then destroyed his writings as he was afraid someone might see them. He still didn't really *want* to do it, but it had started to seem like it might be the only way out. What else could he possibly do? He could think of nothing.

THE LOTTERY

Maybe there was a way out though. There was one thing he could think of to stop this all from happening. He still could become rich. If he did that, then men would envy him. Women would still want him. In fact, Elliot believed it was the *only* way these simple minded women would want him. Then he thought he could lord it over all the stupid men who had vexed him in his past while having a beautiful girlfriend who followed them around like a dog. It wasn't like he really wanted to kill everyone, he just wanted to be happy.

He went home for a visit in March and told his parents everything was wonderful. He was having the best time ever. He lied to his parents about dropping his classes. He believed this would just be one more thing that they could never possibly understand, so why bother to tell them? They would just worry.

When he went back to school, he literally had nothing to do. He had no friends, no girlfriend, no job, and no classes to attend. He didn't even really have any hobbies. But he did have one thing that consumed his time-becoming rich.

He spent his days pacing in his room trying to think of an idea of how to make millions. Others had done it. He could too. He lay on his bed for hours thinking of ways he could manifest his destiny. He could write a fantasy story that could be made into a movie. He could invent something. He could start a business. The problem was all these things would take time, and Elliot needed to become rich right away. Not years from now. What was the point of being rich when he was 30, or even 25? He felt he would never survive in this cruel world if he had to wait so long. He wanted happiness now, not in the distant future. He could think of nothing.

But there was still the lottery. He started watching the Mega Millions jackpot grow. He had saved a lot of money that had been given to him by his parents, so buying a bunch of tickets wouldn't hurt his wallet too much. He spent $50 to $100 dollars on tickets each time he purchased them. He never won, which frustrated him to no end, but no one else was winning either. The jackpot kept rising, which made him even more excited to keep playing. He thought to himself maybe the reason he hadn't won yet was that he was destined to win even more money than he could right now. He fantasized that once he won, he would buy a mansion on the ocean and numerous expensive cars. Possibly even a Lamborghini. Then he would drive back to his old college and watch all those ridiculously stupid girls throw themselves at him.

The jackpot rose to over $290 million. Elliot spent $400 on tickets. He didn't win, but no one else did either. This seemed like it was truly meant to be. It hit $363 million, and he spent $500. But still, no one won. He couldn't believe how much money he was going to win. Then, finally, it hit $657 million, which was the highest jackpot there ever was in the history of Mega Millions. He believed that it was for him to win. All of what had happened in his life, all he had suffered, all the indignities and the pain was just so this could happen. No one deserved it more after all that he had been through. He thought it was fated that he would win.

He spent $700 on tickets. His whole body felt electric with excitement. He spent days fantasizing about the incredible sex he would have with his new, hot girlfriend when he won. She would look deeply into his eyes and tell him how much she loved him. Her body would be his to do anything with that he desired. She would be his minion.

Finally the numbers were drawn, but Elliot couldn't bring himself to check who won right away. It was too important. He waited three days to check the results. He sat in his room and meditated, telling himself over and over that he was a new multimillionaire. He barely ate during this time, and slept little, in fits and starts. Often, he started to pull up the results of the lottery on his laptop, but then shut the page down before he could see who had won.

Finally, when the fourth day came, he forced himself to check to see who won the lottery. He didn't win. He was crushed. Destroyed. Humiliated. Once again he had thought his fate, his destiny, was something different than what it turned out to be. How could this keep happening to him? He thought he wasn't a bad person. He was nice to people, smart, kind, a gentleman. Why couldn't anything ever go his way? He fell into a very dark mood.

This time the depression he felt was worse than ever. He felt life was over. Or maybe it never began. He stayed in his room alone, even over spring break, while all the other guys went off and had fun with their friends and their girlfriends. He thought of all of them on beaches in exotic locations, the dumb jocks throwing a football around while their girlfriends laid on the beach and tanned their perfect bodies. He stayed in his room for an entire month, except when he absolutely had to come out for food or to go to the bathroom. There was no reason for him to do anything.

He tried to contact James a few times to no avail. He was being completely ignored. Finally he called and surprised James by getting him on the phone, but James quickly found a reason to hang up. Elliot wrote James on Facebook to tell him how rude he had been to him. James wrote back and said he didn't want to be friends anymore. He didn't even bother to tell him why. To Elliot this was the worst betrayal imaginable. He had trusted James, and now even he had forsaken him. Elliot had no friends left. No one in the world.

His depression became even worse. His hatred for women ever stronger. But Elliot was a fighter. He wouldn't give up. He kept thinking this had to be some sort of enormous test.

Once again he ruminated and perseverated for days on end on a way that he could become happy, and once again all he could come up with was the thought of becoming wealthy. He would become rich and lose his virginity to a beautiful woman. They would marry and have children, perfect children that would never have the awful life that his parents and society had forced upon him. Then he would have his revenge on all of those foolish enough to think that they were better than him.

He began to read *Power of Your Subconscious Mind,* by Joseph Murphy, which was also based on the Law of Attraction, and began to meditate on winning the lottery. He did this for an entire month. He believed winning the lottery and becoming rich was the only way he would have what he wanted, and if he didn't get that, well, he would be forced to carry out the Day of Retribution. He began to take long walks where he did nothing but concentrate on his vast winnings while he waited for the jackpot to reach $100 million. He didn't want to purchase a ticket before it got that high. He thought that would be a waste.

One summer day, while practicing the power of his subconscious mind in a park, Elliot came across a group of jocks playing kickball, the kind he had despised for his entire life. They were yelling and high fiving each other. Elliot thought they were acting like complete morons. Even worse to him, there was a group of young women watching them play, all of them wearing next to nothing, laying in the grass, showing off their hard stomachs and their firm asses.

Elliot simply couldn't take it anymore. It was just too much for him. He wondered why people continued to do things like this to him?

He seethed with anger. He drove to a local Kmart and purchased a Super Soaker, filled it with orange juice, and went back to the park. They were still there of course, having fun. Elliot thought they were rubbing it in his face how much they had and how little he had. He ran at them, screaming with rage as he sprayed them with orange juice with the Super Soaker. He only wished that he had boiling oil in the Super Soaker instead. The girls lay there and screamed while the boys yelled at him and chased him, but he was too quick. He made it to his car before they caught him. He drove away as fast as he could with his adrenaline pumping. He felt alive.

August arrived and he continued to mediate on the fact that he was to win the Mega Millions jackpot as he had been doing the entire summer. Despite his previous failures he was certain he would win.

At this point one might wonder why Elliot again and again thought he was going to win the lottery, even though he never had done so before, and not only that, each time he tried, things had ended in abject heartbreak. Up until the act of mass murder that Elliot perpetrated, it's by far the biggest sign of how mentally ill he was. Throughout his manifesto he never seems to address how literally insane this thought process was. He just relates each instance of being convinced he was going to win the lottery in the exact same way.

Elliot was to move to another room on the complex for the coming school year. Spencer had a few more girls to his apartment, but Elliot thought they were ugly, so he didn't care all that much. In his mind, Elliot would never stoop so low as to debase himself that way. He thought Spencer was a short, chubby fool who slept with bottom-feeder whores. This was not the life Elliot would ever want for himself, but what he did continue to care about was that Spencer knew how pathetic his own life was. It gnawed at him more each day that, in the entire world, Spencer was the only person who truly knew how little Elliot had in his life, and he hated this. Once he moved he could start all over again, and show his new roomies who he truly was.

Elliot was ambivalent about his new apartment, or who his new roomies would be. He thought he was about to win the lottery after all. He would be living in a mansion soon. No sense getting wound up about silly things. Life is too short.

The jackpot had finally reached $100 million, just like Elliot had been willing it to become. He felt his meditation was working. He believed no one had won yet because the prize was sitting there for Elliot to claim. He began to become more and more excited and visualized himself celebrating after he had won. He was going to do so many amazing things. He couldn't decide whether he would just settle on one beautiful woman to marry, or if he would be better off being a playboy and keeping his own personal harem. He finally bought a ticket. He saw on the news that the winner of the lottery was from California. Elliot knew he had won. It was his destiny.

He didn't though. He checked the ticket over and over again, but the numbers just didn't match up. How could this be? All night he screamed in agony in his tiny room, slashing at the air with a knife before finally crying himself to sleep.

The next day he went to the shooting range and rented a gun. He would need to be at least handy with one when it was time for the Day of Retribution. He only stayed a few minutes, firing the gun at the targets before him, when he began to feel sick to his stomach and left. He felt awful about the whole thing. He wondered to himself why did he have to do this? Why wasn't life fair? Why was he being forced to kill?

After the day at the range, after he lost the millions that were destined to be his and would have changed his life, he spent a lot of time thinking. As he wrote:

> *Within the following days, I spent a lot of time at the park, watching the wind blow through the trees and the children playing in the fields. I questioned*

the very fabric of reality. Why did this all exist? I wondered. How did life come to be? What was the nature of reality? What was my place in all of it? There was no point to my life anymore. I was never going to lose my virginity. I was never going to get a girlfriend. Because girls are repulsed by me, I was never going to have children and pass on my genes. The only way that I could have been worthy enough to beautiful girls is if I become wealthy at a young age, and the faith I had in that happenning had just been crushed. There was no hope left. The life I could have had ceased to exist. I will never have sex, never have love, never have children. I will never be a creator, but I could be a destroyer. Life had been cruel to me. The human species had rejected me all my life, despite the fact that I am the ideal, magnificent gentleman. Life itself is twisted and disgusting, I mused. Humans are brutal animals. If I cannot thrive among them, then I will destroy them all. I didn't want things to turn out this way. I wanted a happy, healthy life of love and sex. But if I'm unable to have such a life, then I will have no choice but to exact revenge on the society that denied it to me.

His new roomies arrived in September. He thought both were nerds, but they were not intimidating to Elliot in the least. One was named Jon, who was an Asian-American, and the other was an American kid named Chris. Both of them just hung out in their rooms all day and played video games, which suited Elliot just fine. He had no interest in being friends with either of them. What would be the point? And since they had no social life either, Elliot didn't feel as ashamed as he did when living with Spencer.

He registered for a few classes just to fool his parents, so they would keep sending him money. He didn't go to any of them. Why bother? He knew he would either be wealthy soon, or he will have enacted the Day of Retribution. Either way, he thought taking classes would be rather silly.

With no outward stimulation whatsoever, Elliot began to completely live in his mind, and what was going on in there wasn't pretty. He spent his days doing nothing but fantasizing about either becoming immensely wealthy, or slaughtering people like the powerful king he felt he was born to be. He wanted to watch the popular jocks who taunted him and the beautiful whores who ignored him run from him in fear and beg him for their lives. He wanted to be a God.

He didn't want his roomies to know he wasn't going to classes, so he spent his days reading books at a library a few towns away. At night he hung out in his room and fantasized about winning the lottery. This was his life.

Everywhere he went he saw young happy couples. He continued to be ignored. They didn't care about his designer clothes or his car. They didn't care that he was a true gentleman. He felt he was nothing. He was ashamed to be seen by others every day.

There was still hope though. He found a new lottery to play. Powerball. The jackpot was well over $500 million, but because it wasn't available in California, Elliot had to drive hours to Arizona to get a ticket. It took him close to ten hours to get there, but what is ten hours when one has spent a lifetime waiting for happiness? Such a small price to pay for extreme riches. It also gave him time to meditate on winning and practice the Law of Attraction. Maybe he just hadn't been doing it right so far. Once he won he hoped he would have his sexy girlfriend; he would be superior to all; he would be able to lord it over all of those who had mocked or ignored him. And win he would. There were no other options.

When he got home after the long drive, he went to bed with the thoughts in his head of being wildly rich. True bliss was right around the corner. It had been so long coming. He literally couldn't wait to feel the feeling of relief, maybe even giddiness when he won. While he went to bed confident, he woke up he feeling like his head was going to explode. His anxiety was through the roof. He looked at the website and saw there were three winners, one from Arizona. Elliot was so relieved. Finally! Why did he get so worried? He knew it was he who had won. It was his destiny.

He had purchased 50 tickets and began to look through them one by one to find the winner. He looked through them all. No winner. He was stunned. He looked again. And again. And again. He hadn't won.

He sat very still for quite a while. He felt dead inside. No, he actually *was* dead, he felt his life was over.

Then he got in his car and drove away aimlessly. As he drove he saw many happy couples walking down the street together, holding hands, smiling at each other, laughing together. He believed now more than ever he could never be one of them. He drove to a park, sat in his car and cried for hours, sobbing hysterically.

He needed to talk to someone, but there was no one who understood him. Since he had no other options, no friends who understood him, or rather, no friends at all, he called his parents, his mother first and then his father. He went on and on about how he was a loser, a virgin, how he had no friends, he was not the type of son that any parent would ever want. How his life was Hell. His parents were both rather upset by this display and decided Elliot should see his psychiatrist when he was home.

Elliot had nothing left. No hope. He started planning the Day of Retribution.

It was time to buy a gun; he purchased a Glock 34 semiautomatic pistol. Once the waiting period ended, he went back to the store to get it and brought it back to his room. He felt different when he held it. More powerful. More alpha. This would certainly have the desired affect more than a hot coffee or a Super Soaker filled with orange juice. At the same time, he needed to be careful. The police aren't really going to care a whole lot about someone being sprayed with orange juice, but if he shot and killed someone, he would go to prison for life. This was unimaginable. He was going to have to be careful.

But nothing really changed. Sure, he had a gun, but he still felt tormented by the world, by women. He stayed in his room perseverating, ruminating. He had been in Santa Barbara for two years and still no girl had fucked him, or even wanted to fuck him, as far as he knew. Sometimes he could even hear them talking outside his window, their voices intermingling with some man they'd chosen over him. He kept getting angrier. More depressed.

As unimaginable as it might seem, once again, Elliot decided he had one chance to get out of this. There was still a way out; he might not have to kill people, there was still Powerball. One must admit Elliot tried so hard. He never gave up. He drove to Arizona again and again, four times in all, over a period of months. Each time he became more and more desperate. It was all he thought he had to live for. The only way he would get a beautiful girlfriend, the only thing to keep him from killing. Each time he didn't win, but he kept trying. Why? Because it was his destiny, or at least he thought it was. If he was wrong, he believed he only had one more destiny to live for. Finally, in March he gave up. He would never have this life he dreamed of.

He bought another handgun. A SIG Sauer P226.

Since he was doing absolutely nothing at school either socially or scholastically, he began to go home on weekends, often spending time with his brother Jazz. While Elliot enjoyed his time with his little brother, it bothered him how athletic Jazz already was, how social he seemed to be. He believed that Jazz was so much luckier than he was in every way.

During the week. when in Isla Vista, he stayed in his room thinking and brooding, questioning why the world was this way. He did this for pretty much every single hour of each moment he was awake. Of course he despised all the men he considered boorish, obnoxious douchebags that he saw all the time, but it was nothing compared to how much he hated the girls that chose to be with them, instead of himself.

He wrote of his thoughts:

> *All I had ever wanted was to love women, but their behavior has only earned my hatred. I want to have sex with them, and make them feel good, but they would be disgusted at the prospect. They have no sexual attraction towards me. It is such an injustice, and I vehemently questioned why things had to be this way. Why do women behave like vicious, stupid, cruel animals who take delight in my suffering and starvation? Why do they have a perverted sexual attraction for the most brutish of men instead of gentlemen of intelligence?*

> *I concluded that women are flawed. There is something mentally wrong with the way their brains are wired, as if they haven't evolved from animal-like thinking. They are incapable of reason or thinking rationally. They are like animals, completely controlled by their primal, depraved emotions and impulses. That is why they are attracted to barbaric, wild, beast-like men. They are beasts themselves. Beasts should not be able to have any rights in a civilized society. If their wickedness is not contained, the whole of humanity will be held back from advancement to a more civilized state. Women should not have the right to choose who to mate with. That choice should be made for them by civilized men of intelligence. If women had the freedom to choose which men to mate with, like they do today, they would breed with*

stupid, degenerate men, which would only produce stupid, degenerate offspring. This in turn would hinder the advancement of humanity. Not only hinder it, but devolve humanity completely. Women are like a plague that must be quarantined. When I came to this brilliant, perfect revelation, I felt like everything was now clear to me, in a bitter, twisted way. I am one of the few people on this world who has the intelligence to see this. I am like a god, and my purpose is to exact ultimate Retribution on all of the impurities I see in the world.

Elliot started to spend time on a website called PUAhate. com, which stood for Pickup Artist Hate. As one might imagine, it was a website forum for those men who not only never had received any attention from the opposite sex but were extremely angry about it. This was a website for incels before the word really existed in the mainstream, or at least was widely known.

To people on this site, women only go out with Chads, handsome guys with big muscles, who have a ton of money, and everyone else is left to drown in despair. As Elliot read the posts on the site from other men such as himself, he became even more convinced of how evil women were. Before it seemed to him like he was the only one who had suffered so much, but now he thought there were numerous men out there all with the same problem, purely because most alpha men are animals, and the women who follow them are shallow, ridiculous fools.

He tried to show the website to his parents to help them understand why he was so miserable, but neither of them ever responded to him. Who knows what they thought? He often urged others on the site to fight back writing, "One day incels will realize their true strength and numbers and will overthrow this oppressive feminist system. Start envisioning a world where WOMEN FEAR YOU."

Summer had come. Elliot hated summer more than all the other seasons because that was when women would be showing off their bodies even more so than usual, while ignoring Elliot just as much as usual. Not a good combination for his already fragile mental health. Just seeing the tan body of a hot woman was enough to send him into a rage, often followed by tears.

It was time. He needed revenge. He was special. A gentleman among idiots. Yet he was ignored by every woman he had ever met. Not one girl had ever wanted him. He wasn't invited to even one single party. He began to fantasize more and more about carrying out his plans of attack. He didn't want to die. Of course it would be better to carry out these acts and survive and live like a king, but in reality he knew he would be captured and imprisoned if he enacted his plans. So he began to prepare to kill himself.

He wanted to kill as many hot, young women as possible, so he decided on Isla Vista, as there were plentiful gorgeous girls and couples that irritated him there all the time. Of course, since this was also his home base, it made things so much easier as well. All he had to do was walk out his front door, and he would see numerous people he wanted to make his victims. Although in his mind, he was the victim. He couldn't wait to turn from tormented to tormentor.

He thought of doing it on Halloween as there were tons of people around drunk, which would make them easy targets. He could easily disguise himself in some random Halloween costume, which would make escape much easier, but there would be cops everywhere, much more than usual because of the holiday. He decided on November 2013 instead. He worried about the fact that he would die, but without a beautiful blonde to have sex with, he already felt dead. It was much scarier to him to think of going on with life this way as opposed to thinking about dying. He felt he had no other way out. He was never going to become rich.

When he went for walks as he did often, he saw other young men hanging out with gorgeous women who weren't nearly as good looking as he thought he was. None of it made any sense. He believed if only one hot girl had ever looked at him, asked him out, kissed him none of this ever would have happened.

Elliot could still get joy, or at least a semblance of it, from some things. A beautiful beach, a sumptuous meal, an amazing view from the top of a mountain, those things still moved him. He didn't want to totally give up. He still had five more months until November. Five more months to save himself, to save the world.

His mother bought a house. It was in a decent area, and it had a pool. Yet Elliot was still angry that she had never married someone rich, as she obviously could have. She was beautiful, at least when she was younger, and had dated many rich and successful men. He considered her very selfish in not helping him this way. It could have changed everything for him. He felt that numerous people were going to die, and his mother would lose her only son, all because she didn't do the right thing. It was ridiculous.

His parents hired some social skills counselors to work with Elliot. They were paid to hang out with him and teach him how to talk to people and act around them. One was a young man named Karlin. He was nice to Elliot; they spent time walking around Isla Vista together and talking. It went well until Elliot asked him if he had ever had sex with anyone in Isla Vista. Karlin said yes, that he had sex with four girls in his time there. Elliot was enraged. He believed Karlin was average looking, and this upset Elliot even more. He didn't see him again after that. He was trying to feel better, not worse.

The other counselor was a pretty, blonde girl named Sasha. Elliot felt pathetic that his parents hired a girl to hang out with him, but since it was the only girl he had spent time with in years, he couldn't say no. He had to admit he had a good time with her, but it made him feel that he was hiring a prostitute of sorts. In his mind, she obviously would never spend time with him if she wasn't being paid to do so.

He decided he still was going to give the world one more chance. He had mercy for others, even though he felt they didn't deserve it.

In July he began exercising like mad to tone his body, so he would be attractive to the girls in Isla Vista. He would give women another opportunity to be with him. But if they shunned him, if he still was a virgin, and if he was still alone in November, he would have no choice but to enact his vengeance.

THE PARTY

July 20, 2013, was just a few days before Elliot turned 22. He decided to go out in Isla Vista in an attempt to lose his virginity before his birthday. Elliot always hated birthdays; they were always a stark reminder of how awful things had become for him. Birthdays, Valentine's Day, New Year's Eve, all were days in which he was forced to pay attention to how horrific his life was.

He was anxious and needed to work up his courage to be around people, so he bought some vodka and slugged a good portion of it down before he went out. It seemed to help. He felt looser, more open, more capable.

He saw a large house party on his travels and walked right in like he owned the place. That's how drunk he was.

He thought it was awful of course, just a huge party filled with jerks, the types of people Elliot despised. Rap music was blaring; people were playing beer pong and chugging beers, all the things these annoying savages did and that he, a true gentleman, disliked. But no matter. He was in, at the party, and so were many gorgeous girls. He decided he could slum it, just this once. This could be his night.

There were around 100 people at the party. It was big enough so that Elliot would not stand out as not knowing anyone and could walk around unmolested by whoever the party's hosts were. But he didn't want to just fit in, he wanted to be noticed, in fact he wanted to get laid, and that simply was not happening. He tried to act like he belonged.

He drank beer, and he tried to mingle, but no one paid any attention to him at all. When he stood next to beautiful women, they either kept chattering away to whoever they were already talking to or just acted really awkward until he walked away.

Soon he saw a short Asian guy who was not particularly attractive talking to a gorgeous white girl. This made him angry. He thought to himself, "How could an ugly Asian attract the attention of a white girl, while a beautiful Eurasian like myself never had any attention from them?" Of course Elliot himself wasn't attracted to Asians; he didn't even particularly like brunettes. All he wanted were tall blondes that looked like models, but this irony seemed to escape him. In fact, if he were standing at this party as drunk as he was, and a short, average looking Asian girl came up and talked to him he almost certainly would have blown her off.

He walked up to them and bumped into the man on purpose and started acting like a jerk to him and the girl he was with, attempting to make a scene. He was so drunk that they just felt pity for him and looked at him with concern in their eyes. They told him he should get water as he seemed super wasted and asked him if he was okay.

This made him even angrier how they were patronizing him like he was some socially inept loser. He went drunkenly out to the front yard, almost falling over most of the way there, but not before he hurled one last feeble insult at the man.

He was all by himself in the front yard. So as not to look ridiculous, he climbed up on a ledge that was on the edge of the lawn that bordered the street. It was about ten feet off the ground all told. He saw many couples walking by. Elliot stood on the ledge and pointed his hand at them as if it were a gun and pretended to shoot at them, laughing at the top of his lungs.

Other people at the party came out to the lawn and saw him on the ledge, so they climbed up too. One might think that Elliot had finally been thought of as a leader. He was the first one on the ledge after all, but no, all the boys ignored him, and all the girls acted like he didn't exist. Elliot began to loudly insult the group beside him, calling them names in a belligerent manner, but they did not care. They just insulted him back, and even worse, did so while laughing at him, like he posed no threat to them at all.

He lost it. He screamed that he would kill them all. In a rage, he attempted to push the girls off the ledge one by one, but just like all his plans, up to this point anyway, it didn't work out. He didn't manage to push even one girl over, in fact, one of the jocks on the ledge rather easily pushed him off instead. When he hit the ground, he felt his ankle snap. His first instinct was to get away, and despite the blind pain he tried to escape, to stumble down the street.

But then he realized that he had lost his Gucci sunglasses. This simply would not do. He loved them so. He had to get them back. He turned and stumbled back to the party; except he was so drunk, he wound up at the wrong house, which didn't stop him from aggressively demanding his sunglasses back. This did not work out well in large part because no one had any idea what he was talking about. He was called a "pussy" and things of that nature, which of course caused Elliot to be even more verbally aggressive. A bit of a brawl started, during which Elliot got off one punch before he was dragged to the ground and punched and kicked before some people broke up the fight enough for Elliot to escape.

While he had been mocked and bullied numerous times in his life, he had never actually been beaten up although there is little doubt that after attempting to throw women off a ten-foot ledge and drunkenly accusing strangers of stealing from him, he certainly did have it coming.

Nevertheless he felt humiliated. How could this have happened to him? In his mind he had gone to the party to lose his virginity to a beautiful woman, and instead he was beaten by a group of vicious thugs. He wondered why no one cared about his misery. Not one girl offered to help him as he struggled home broken and bloody. Worse, no one was attracted to him. No one offered to have sex with him to make him feel better. No beautiful girl tucked him into bed and kissed him on the forehead.

That night, he drunkenly called his parents in anguish. He even called his sister, who he didn't even like. He realized his gold chain was gone, and believed that whichever person took it from him would be selling it to purchase drugs. It was too much to bear.

The next day, he couldn't walk at all. He also was in a panic. After all he had threatened to kill many people, and he had tried to push girls off a ledge. This attention could ruin everything. He wasn't supposed to out himself as a future mass murderer. Not yet anyway.

His father picked him up and took him to the hospital. He talked to the police, as did the others involved in the incident, but stories didn't match, and Elliot never heard anything about it again. Elliot said he was victimized, but many witnesses said something quite different. In a town like Isla Vista, this was probably just one of numerous drunken skirmishes on that particular evening.

In the police report about the incident, Elliot said he never tried to push anyone, but admitted he called one of the subjects "ugly" before he was pushed over a ten-foot ledge. Then, while sitting on a chair on the lawn, he said ten male subjects approached him and called him a faggot before beating him up.

The officer who took the report didn't believe him. He described him as shy, timid, and not forthcoming. The report also stated a witness said Elliot had in fact attempted to push two women off the ledge, and his demeanor was "strange."

Elliot's leg was broken, and he had to wear a cast for six weeks. At least it was his left leg, so he still could drive. He spent his 22nd birthday alone at his mother's house. He was now not only a virgin; he was a cripple as well.

In his mind there was no turning back. This was the final straw. He gave them all an opportunity to love him and adore him, but they mocked him and beat him like a dog instead.

As Elliot wrote:

> *The highly unjust experience of being beaten and humiliated in front of everyone in Isla Vista, and their subsequent lack of concern for my well-being, was the last and final straw. I actually gave them all one last chance to accept me, to give me a reason not to hate them, and they devastatingly blew it back in my face. I gave the world too many chances. It was time for Retribution.*

He ended up needing surgery on his leg, when it was completed he needed to have his leg elevated at all times for a whole week. His mother and sister had to go off to Hawaii for a vacation immediately after the surgery. The trip had been planned for months, and Elliot had been invited, but had refused to go. It seemed to be a bad idea for Elliot to stay at his mother's house all alone while they were gone, so he asked his father if he could stay at his house. Soumaya had one of her relatives staying for the summer, so she said "No." Elliot couldn't believe it. His mother put him up at Extended Stay America for a week.

He spent that week thinking about what was to come. He wrote:

> *I felt so shocked and overwhelmed upon realizing that it was definitely going to resort to this. I was going to die soon, and that in itself was hard to accept. I didn't want to die, but I would have no choice. Vengeance is the only path; all other paths had been closed shut. I thought it to be such a tragedy that I was actually going to wage war against women and all of humanity. But then again, women's rejection of me was a declaration*

of war. They insulted me by deeming me inferior of their love and sex. They hate me, and I will return that hatred one-thousand fold. I will inflict suffering on everyone in Isla Vista, just like they have made me suffer. In the past, I have always been at their mercy, and I was given none. On the Day of Retribution, everyone will be at my mercy, and in turn I will show them no mercy at all. My Retribution will be so devastating that it will shake the very foundations of the world.

The injury set back the Day of Retribution a bit, it would be October at the earliest before he would be able to walk without pain. He wouldn't be able to train properly, and he wouldn't be able to get his mind in the right place. He felt he had to be at his absolute peak physically, emotionally, and mentally. There was no telling what might happen.

He couldn't do it in November; he would never be correctly prepared. It would have to be the spring of 2014 before he unleashed his vengeance.

Still, Elliot remained somewhat optimistic. Perhaps something would happen in this time period that would give him a way out of it all. He certainly hoped he wasn't forced into such a thing. When his mother returned from Hawaii, he moved back in with her and spent his time there recuperating. He didn't go out by himself for any reason, he was too humiliated to be seen in public as a cripple.

His parents arranged for him to see his psychiatrist while he was home. Both of his parents as well as Soumaya were there. Much of the session was spent on whether it was okay for Soumaya to not let Elliot stay at her home while he was injured, instead of focusing on what was really going on with Elliot, which of course was rather disturbing. In retrospect, these family concerns seem a tad petty when considering Elliot was planning a mass slaughter. One must admit that

Elliot was quite the master at not letting his parents know his inner thoughts.

He was prescribed Risperidone, which is a medication usually used to treat schizophrenia, bipolar disorder, or irritability associated with autism. Elliot never took the medication, nor did he ever see his psychiatrist again.

Soon he could walk without crutches, and his mother said he needed to go back to school. Elliot had only signed up for a couple of online classes, but he neglected to tell her that. So it was back to Santa Barbara. His roomies Jon and Chris had moved out which saddened Elliot a bit, not that he cared about either of them, but at least they had left him alone.

During a visit home he went to his father's house and had a conversation with Soumaya. She told Elliot that Jazz had signed with an agent as a child actor and that he would be very successful by the time he was Elliot's age. Not only that, but Soumaya said he would probably do very well with women too when he became older.

Elliot decided then he would have to kill Jazz on the Day of Retribution as much as it pained him. He liked Jazz, and even more so liked that Jazz looked up to him, but he thought it would be awful to have his younger brother do everything better than Elliot could. Of course he would probably have to kill Soumaya too, but that would not be difficult, he might even actually enjoy that. He could imagine the surprised look on her face as she took her last breath.

It made things more complicated though. He couldn't kill his father. He would have to kill Soumaya and Jazz at some point when Peter was away on business. Even thinking of such things made him feel sick.

His mother bought him a BMW 3 Series Coupe, which made him feel more confident although he felt she should have purchased him a car such as this years ago. If she had, things might have been better for him, and girls would have found him more attractive. Maybe, just maybe, his new expensive car would help him succeed with women, and the Day of Retribution wouldn't happen. He tried to throw himself into life on the hopes that something, anything would change.

Elliot had two new housemates. In his words:

> They were two foreign Asian students who attended UCSB. These were the biggest nerds I had ever seen, and they were both very ugly with annoying voices. My last two housemates, Chris and Jon, were nerds as well, but at least they were friendly and pleasant. These two new ones were utterly repulsive, and one of them had a very rebellious demeanor about him. He went out of his way to start arguments with me whenever I raised the issue of the noise he made. Hell, even living with Spencer was more pleasant than these two. I knew that when the Day of Retribution came, I would have to kill my housemates to get them out of the way. If they were pleasant to live with, I would regret having to kill them, but due to their behavior I now had no regrets about such a prospect. In fact, I'd even enjoy stabbing them both to death while they slept.

A few months before the Day of Retribution, Elliot had one of the roomies, Cheng Yuan Hong, arrested for stealing a pair of candles from his room. Elliot called 911 to report the theft. The candles were worth around 22 dollars and Elliot placed Hong under citizen's arrest before the police arrived. Elliot said Hong had entered his room and stolen the candles, then refused to return them.

Hong told detectives Elliot had taken some of his rice bowls, which Elliot denied. The case was later dismissed.

One day when he was home visiting his mother's house, he heard his sister's boyfriend Samuel having sex with her through her bedroom door. Samuel was half Mexican, and Elliot considered him a jerk. To listen to his sister moan while having sex with him was almost too much to handle. Samuel didn't even have a car, and he was fucking Elliot's sister. He couldn't believe it.

Nothing had changed. Boys who had much worse cars still had hot women in their passenger seat while Elliot, despite his BMW, did not. One evening, he drove to a secluded area to watch the sunset. Elliot had always loved sunsets, and this one was particularly gorgeous. He ruminated on life, how it was so cruel to him, how he wished that he didn't have to do what he was about to do.

His winter break was uneventful. His mother had taken off to England with his sister and her boyfriend. He attended a Christmas party with his father where he saw numerous people that he knew since he was a child. They all asked him how he was, how was school, how was life. He had nothing to say. He felt he had nothing to be proud of.

On New Year's Eve he drank one of his mother's bottles of wine as he stayed at her house alone. He knew others his age were out partying, having fun. It was okay though; his fun was coming. He felt excitement at this thought.

New Year's Day came. It was 2014. This would be Elliot's last year. He wrote:

> *I had been rejected, insulted, humiliated, cast out, bullied, starved, tortured, and ridiculed for far too long. Humanity is a cruel and brutal species, and the only thing I could do to even the score was to return that cruelty one-thousand fold. Women's rejection of me is a declaration of war, and if it's war they want, then war they shall have. It will be a war that will result in their complete and utter annihilation. I will deliver a blow to my enemies that will be so catastrophic it will redefine the very essence of human nature.*

There are a lot of people that think about doing a lot of messed up things in life, but most of them, almost all of them, don't follow through. It's one thing to fantasize about doing something violent, or robbing a bank, or having sex with your wife's sister, but that's why they are called fantasies. People don't act on them.

Elliot had been thinking of this, dreaming about punishing people like a god, for a long time. And as unbelievable as it may seem, he was about to do it.

Over 2013 and 2014, Elliot went to counseling almost 30 times. He also continued to see Gavin, his life coach. A psychological report from this time suggested that Elliot should enter a residential treatment facility because of his great difficulty integrating with his peers and the rage he showed toward couples, but nothing came of it. He also was prescribed Xanax, which he took irregularly.

Still no one had any idea what was really going inside of the mind of Elliot Rodger. He thought of doing the Day of Retribution on Valentine's Day as he hated that day with a passion, but it was too soon to get organized. He didn't have enough time. He settled on Saturday, April 26, 2014.

He spent the first few months of 2014 trying to enjoy himself, as they were to be the last of his life. He took in beautiful sunsets, went on hikes, walked the beach. He even signed on for a few classes at Santa Barbara City College, but he dropped them after a few weeks. But as he did all these things, he saw happy couples everywhere. He knew it was time.

THE BEST LAID PLANS

Elliot's plan went something like this.

The day prior to the Day of Retribution he would kill as many people as he could by luring them into his apartment, which would be turned into his personal torture chamber. First he would kill his roommates to get them out of the way, which he wasn't excited by, but not depressed about either, as he hated them so. Then he would trick people into entering his apartment and knock them out with a hammer. He would torture those that were particularly good looking as they deserved the pain the most. He would pour boiling water over them and flay them, then cut off their heads once they finally died. He would then put their heads in a bag. He had big plans for his bag of heads down the road.

On the Day of Retribution itself, he would start his War on Women. His plan was to launch an attack on the Alpha Phi Sorority, as he considered it to be the place with the hottest women in Isla Vista. He knew exactly where it was, mostly because he sat outside of it all the time staring at the members of the sorority as they came and went, waiting to be noticed, all to no avail. They would notice him now. This was for certain. He would sneak into their house at night and kill every single one of them. The last thing any of them would see would be his face.

He would then go kill his little brother and Soumaya and take the family SUV. As he was escaping from the cops, he would use his SUV to run over and splatter all sorts of his enemies on his way to Del Playa Street.

Then, as he wrote:

> *Once I reach Del Playa Street, I will dump the bag of severed heads I had saved from my previous victims, proclaiming to everyone how much I've made them all suffer. Once they see all of their friend's heads roll onto the street, everyone will fear me as the powerful god I am. I will then start massacring everyone on Del Playa Street. I will pull up next to a house party and fire bullets at everyone partying on the front yard. I will specifically target the good looking people, and all of the couples. After I have destroyed a house party, I will continue down Del Playa, destroying everything and everyone. When I see the first police car come to their rescue, I will drive away as fast as I can, shooting and ramming anyone in my path until I find a suitable place to finally end my life.*

The bag of heads really seemed important to him somehow.

His plan on ending his life was to swallow a bunch of Xanax and Vicodin along with drinking a bunch of booze, then shoot himself in the head with both of his guns. This needed to go perfectly. It had to. He only had one chance at it. To fail and to be put into prison was simply unfathomable. This was his worst nightmare.

One day while taking a hike together, Elliot told Peter that he had been writing a lot of his thoughts down as of late, so Peter asked his son if he could read it. Elliot just said, "Oh, no, no, no. I'll send it to you soon enough."

The week before the Day of Retribution, he started uploading videos to YouTube to express his views. He knew he was going to be famous soon after all, and he wanted people to know why he chose to do this, without quite getting into detail about what he was going to do.

In the videos Elliot truly hammed it up. While he thought he was being cool, watching them now shows a man who is truly unhinged; one who has no idea how he appears to others.

He winked at the camera, and bobbed his head rhythmically to bouncy songs like "Walking on Sunshine" to show the world how odd it was women didn't find him attractive. As he wrote:

> *I titled one of the videos I uploaded "Why do girls hate me so much?" in which I ask the entire population of women the question I've wanted to ask them for so many years. Why do they hate me so much? Why have they never fancied me? Why do they give their love and sex to other men, but not me, even though I deserve them more? In the video, I show that I am the perfect, magnificent gentleman, worthy of having a beautiful girlfriend, making the world see how unreasonable it is that I've had to struggle all my life to get a girlfriend. It is my attempt to reason with the female gender, to ask them why they have mistreated me.*

Of course the video did not show he was the perfect, magnificent gentleman who is worthy of having a beautiful girlfriend. In fact, he seemed like a complete lunatic.

He continued to post on PUA.Hate.com and other sites of that nature, where he was often mocked by other posters as being pretentious, bitter, and whiny. In response, he would write things such as "I am a drop-dead gorgeous, fabulous, stylish, an exotic gem among thousands of rocks."

One person saw one of Elliot's videos on a site called bodybuilding.com and wrote: "I'm not trying to be mean, but the creepy vibe that you give off in those videos is likely the major reason that you can't get girls." Another said he had a Patrick Bateman vibe.

Elliot continued to upload videos onto YouTube. He was saving his final video for right before his massacre, as he knew it gave up way too much information about his plans. Other than the "Why do girls hate me so much?" video, he put up many others. One is of him and Jazz at the beach, and another features him taking a walk through a park. One is called "Being lonely on Spring Break sucks" while another was titled "My morning drive to school," which is the one that uses the song "Walking on Sunshine" as the soundtrack.

He put up another called "I'm Awesome," which attempts to show Elliot as being good looking, wealthy, and sophisticated. Another, "Dancing in the car, Elliot Rodger style," uses the Whitney Houston song "How Will I Know" in the background. Another one is titled, "Life Is So Unfair Because Girls Don't Want Me." Each one of these videos is totally bizarre in its own way.

He thought maybe some girl would see one of these videos and contact him and tell him how attractive he was, maybe go on a date with him, maybe she would even end his virginity once and for all. If one young woman did, perhaps the Day of Retribution would have never happened. But of course no one responded, except some guys who mocked him.

On April 24, two days before the fateful day, Elliot woke up with an awful cold. This would just not do. He couldn't do all he needed to do if he was ill. His father also had come home for a trip early, and Elliot didn't feel able to kill his father. It just didn't feel right. So he put it off until May 24. Part of him felt relieved. As much as he felt ready, he wasn't sure he wanted to die just yet. Not because he loved life, but because he was afraid of dying.

He promised himself though. May 24 was it. The Day of Retribution was his only purpose in life. He was ready. He could do it.

He thought that at least after he died, people would read his words in his manifesto. Perhaps they would even help change the world. Maybe his acts could change all the injustice and suffering faced by so many.

In his manifesto he wrote:

> *The ultimate evil behind sexuality is the human female. They are the main instigators of sex. They control which men get it and which men don't. Women are flawed creatures, and my mistreatment at their hands has made me realize this sad truth. There is something very twisted and wrong with the way their brains are wired. They think like beasts, and in truth, they are beasts. Women are incapable of having morals or thinking rationally. They are completely controlled by their depraved emotions and vile sexual impulses. Because of this, the men who do get to experience the pleasures of sex and the privilege of breeding are the men who women are sexually attracted to… the stupid, degenerate, obnoxious men. I have observed this all my life. The most beautiful of women choose to mate with the most brutal of men, instead of magnificent gentlemen like myself.*

> *Women should not have the right to choose who to mate and breed with. That decision should be made for them by rational men of intelligence. If women continue to have rights, they will only hinder the advancement of the human race by breeding with degenerate men and creating stupid, degenerate offspring. This will cause humanity to become even more depraved with each generation. Women have more power in human society than they deserve, all because of sex. There is no creature more evil and depraved than the human female.*

Women are like a plague. They don't deserve to have any rights. Their wickedness must be contained in order prevent future generations from falling to degeneracy. Women are vicious, evil, barbaric animals, and they need to be treated as such.

In fully realizing these truths about the world, I have created the ultimate and perfect ideology of how a fair and pure world would work. In an ideal world, sexuality would not exist. It must be outlawed. In a world without sex, humanity will be pure and civilized. Men will grow up healthily, without having to worry about such a barbaric act. All men will grow up fair and equal, because no man will be able to experience the pleasures of sex while others are denied it. The human race will evolve to an entirely new level of civilization, completely devoid of all the impurity and degeneracy that exists today.

In order to completely abolish sex, women themselves would have to be abolished. All women must be quarantined like the plague they are, so that they can be used in a manner that actually benefits a civilized society. In order to carry this out, there must exist a new and powerful type of government, under the control of one divine ruler, such as myself. The ruler that establishes this new order would have complete control over every aspect of society, in order to direct it towards a good and pure place. At the disposal of this government, there needs to be a highly trained army of fanatically loyal troops, in order to enforce such revolutionary laws.

The first strike against women will be to quarantine all of them in concentration camps. At these camps, the vast majority of the female population will be deliberately starved to death. That would be an efficient and fitting way to kill them all off. I would take great pleasure and satisfaction in condemning every single woman on earth to starve to death. I would have an enormous tower built just for myself, where I can oversee the entire concentration camp and gleefully watch them all die. If I can't have them, no one will, I'd imagine thinking to myself as I oversee this. Women represent everything that is unfair with this world, and in order to make the world a fair place, they must all be eradicated.

A few women would be spared, however, for the sake of reproduction. These women would be kept and bred in secret labs. There, they will be artificially inseminated with sperm samples in order to produce offspring. Their depraved nature will slowly be bred out of them in time.

Future generations of men would be oblivious to these remaining women's existence, and that is for the best. If a man grows up without knowing of the existence of women, there will be no desire for sex. Sexuality will completely cease to exist. Love will cease to exist. There will no longer be any imprint of such concepts in the human psyche. It is the only way to purify the world.

In such a pure world, the man's mind can develop to greater heights than ever before. Future generations will live their lives free of having to worry about the barbarity of sex and women, which will enable them to expand their intelligence and advance the human race to a state of perfect civilization.

Elliot Rodger had totally lost his mind.

Something almost messed up the whole plan.

One day he heard a knock on his door. When he opened it, he saw a group of police officers staring back at him. Elliot was instantly terrified. If they searched his room, they would find his guns; they would find his writings about his plans. He would go to jail. He would make the news. He would be a joke and a failure.

It turns out his mother had seen the videos, became very disturbed at their content, and called a mental health agency, who in turn called the police. The police told Elliot it was his mother who called them, but she denied it when Elliot talked to her later. Elliot quickly became more relaxed when he realized that all the police wanted to know was whether Elliot was suicidal. And of course he convinced them he wasn't fairly quickly. It was all one big misunderstanding.

In reality, he was just a little suicidal, but only after he was going to slaughter all sorts of people. If there is one thing that is inarguable about Elliot Rodger it is that he was an extremely good liar.

The police called Elliot's mother while they were there. Elliot was calm, shy, and polite, and just said he was lonely and having a difficult time. He was having trouble fitting in socially in Isla Vista. The videos were merely a way of expressing himself. There was nothing that gave deputies reason to believe he was a danger to himself or others.

He said his mother was a "worrywart."

Investigators later wrote: "During this welfare check, the suspect did not show any signs of being, or make any statements indicating, that he was a danger to himself or others in retrospect, this was one of several examples of the suspect's ability to present a normal affect when interacting with others."

Elliot later wrote to someone online who asked him what happened to the videos he had seen. Elliot said he had taken them down because his parents saw them. He said he would put more up within a few days.

Around 9:30 p.m. on May 23, 2014, Peter Rodger received an e-mail from his son. .Before he could read it the phone rang, it was Chin. She told him, "You've got to go on YouTube right away." Peter did and saw the videos of his son saying horrible, terrible things and felt his heart go dark.

In the video Elliot said:

> *Hi. Elliot Rodger here. Well, this is my last video, it has all had to come to this. Tomorrow is the Day of Retribution, the day in which I will have my revenge against humanity, against all of you. For the last eight years of my life, ever since I hit puberty, I've been forced to endure an existence of loneliness, rejection, and unfulfilled desires all because girls have never been attracted to me. Girls gave their affection, and sex and love to other men but never to me.*

> *I'm 22 years old, and I'm still a virgin. I've never even kissed a girl. I've been through college for two and a half years, more than that actually, and I'm still a virgin. It has been very torturous. College is the time when everyone experiences those things such as sex and fun and pleasure. Within those years, I've had to rot in loneliness. It's not fair.*

> *You girls have never been attracted to me. I don't know why you girls aren't attracted to me, but I will punish you all for it. It's an injustice, a crime, because... I don't know what you don't see in me. I'm the perfect guy, and yet you throw yourselves*

at these obnoxious men instead of me, the supreme gentleman.

I will punish all of you for it. (laughs) On the Day of Retribution I'm going to enter the hottest sorority house of UCSB. And I will slaughter every spoiled, stuck-up, blonde slut I see inside there. All those girls I've desired so much, they would have all rejected me and looked down upon me as an inferior man if I ever made a sexual advance towards them (scoffs) while they throw themselves at these obnoxious brutes. I'll take great pleasure in slaughtering all of you.

You will finally see that I am in truth the superior one. The true alpha male. (laughs) Yes. After I've annihilated every single girl in the sorority house, I will take to the streets of Isla Vista and slay every single person I see there. All those popular kids who live such lives of hedonistic pleasures while I've had to rot in loneliness for all these years. They've all looked down upon me every time I tried to go out and join them. They've all treated me like a mouse.

Well now I will be a god compared to you. You will all be animals. You are animals, and I will slaughter you like animals. And I will be a god. Exacting my retribution on all those who deserve it. You do deserve it. Just for the crime of living a better life than me. All you popular kids, you've never accepted me, and now you will all pay for it. And girls, all I ever wanted was to love you, and to be loved by you. I've wanted a girlfriend, I've wanted sex, I've wanted love, affection, adoration. You think I'm unworthy of it. That's a crime that can never be forgiven.

If I can't have you, girls, I will destroy you. (laughs) You denied me a happy life, and in turn, I will deny all of you life. (laughs) It's only fair.

I hate all of you. Humanity is a disgusting, wretched, depraved species. If I had it in my power, I would stop at nothing (points finger at camera) to reduce every single one of you to mountains of skulls and rivers of blood. And rightfully so.

You deserve to be annihilated, and I'll give that to you. You never showed me any mercy, and so I will show you none. (laughs)

You've forced me to suffer all my life, and now I'll force you all suffer. I've waited a long time for this. I'll give you exactly what you deserve. All of you. All you girls who rejected me and looked down upon me and you know, treated me like scum while you gave yourselves to other men. And all of you men, for living a better life than me, all of you sexually active men, I hate you. I hate all of you. I can't wait to give you exactly what you deserve. Utter annihilation. (laughs)

Elliot had sent his manifesto to his mother, father, life coach, and a few others. It was called *My Twisted World*. When Chin saw it, she read it briefly, then went to her son's YouTube channel that she had been monitoring and saw a video titled "Elliot Rodger's Retribution" in which he sat in the Black BMW she gave to him and watched him promise the world that he would slaughter people for what had been done to him.

Chin and Peter got in his car and drove as fast as they could to Isla Vista, 100 miles away, only to hear on the radio the early reports of a mass shooting in that area. Peter later said, "I didn't know what he was doing. I just wanted to go and find him...and talk to him, do something. You know, hold him. You know, talk reason." He kept hitting redial on his phone over and over again, trying to call Elliot, but there was no answer.

They began reading stories on their phones of an active shooter involving a black BMW. They got on the phone with the sheriff's department and told them who they were. They were soon directed to a Home Depot parking lot in the area where they were to await further instructions.

Soon, a sheriff pulled into the parking lot where they were waiting and said to them: "We've found a deceased person, and we found a license in his pocket that fits your son's description."

Peter was confused and said, "Can somebody clarify this to me?"

The sheriff said again, "We've found a deceased person, and we found a license in his pocket that fits your son's description."

Elliot Rodger was dead.

AFTERWORD

Elliot Rodger certainly didn't have quite the affect he was hoping for with his Day of Retribution. One has to wonder what was going through his mind in his final moments. What he accomplished was a disaster compared to what he hoped it would be. This was not what he planned.

He didn't lure people into his apartment and torture them for hours; he didn't kill all the most beautiful women in his chosen sorority, and he didn't change how the world looks at women. He didn't become thought of as powerful. In fact most people, if they've heard of him at all, think of him as a bit of a joke.

But he did become a bit of an icon for a certain group of people. Incels.

Since his death there have been many online incel communities that have touted Elliot as the "Supreme Gentleman" and lauded his actions. One must of course remember that much like many other online groups full of young people, the incel community is full of trolls. Who is to know how many truly hail Elliot Rodger as a hero and how many are just messing around and trying to get a rise out of each other, and also out of those who read books such as these. But there is no doubt a small segment of incels looked at him as someone to respect, and perhaps even emulate.

That's really the thing about Internet culture. One would be truly naïve to look at words that people say in chat rooms and on websites and truly believe everything they say. That's kind of the whole point of the dark corners of the Web. One can say whatever one wants. Whether joking, screwing with people's minds, or trying to make oneself appear different than they truly are, who is to stop them? Much of the Internet is about gamesmanship. Someone says something truly odd and messed up, and then someone else tries to top it.

But when looking at the mainstream media, and to what many people think, incels are dangerous as a whole, and are to be feared. And that makes sense in some way. Elliot Rodger thought he deserved love. He thought a woman should want to have sex with him. He was entitled to it. And when that didn't happen, he got very angry, and he did something about it; although what he did made pretty much zero sense at all.

Some in the incel community call him a hero for what he did. Again, one must be careful to think that all these people were serious, but still, to even write such a thing, or say it out loud, that a person doing what Elliot did was heroic, should give one pause.

Some call him "Saint Elliot" and talk about committing a violent attack as "Going E.R." On message boards, May 23 has been called St. Elliot's Day." In one Reddit thread posted the same day, one person wrote: "May he rest in peace. Let us not be sad. Today is a day to celebrate... the retribution."

Some think his manifesto, which was used for background detail for this book, is a work of genius, something to follow, something that speaks to them. Women are responsible for their misery, and only violence can make things right. This is known as "Aggrieved entitlement," the suggestion that their situation is unjust and violence through revenge is justified. Sex is a basic human right for all men, and women who deny that to men are committing a crime.

On one message board a user wrote: "All violence, random attacks and terrorism are done by men who cannot find GFs, and thus women are DIRECTLY responsible for all of it. The ONLY way to fix this problem is to take away women's rights and adopt a system of equal redistribution of women."

A report by the Southern Poverty Law Center named Elliot as the "first alt-right killer." They name many others that they believed had followed in his footsteps.

I asked Serge, the administrator of Incels.Is what he thought of Elliot and others who have killed and thought to be under the "influence" of the Incel movement. He replied:

> *Inceldom is not a movement, it's a situation. There is no incel political agenda nor inclination. Elliot Rodger was a mentally ill man who was in therapy since he was 9, didn't take his antipsychotic medication, had no real friends, felt alienated at home due to family problems, and was allowed to purchase guns and show hateful behavior without repercussions. In short, his status as incel was exaggerated by media, but even if you wish to call him one, clearly there were more serious issues behind his rampage. Being single doesn't automatically make you hate people, as he did.*

In fact, Elliot never mentions the word "incel" in his manifesto although he did mention it once on a bodybuilding site, saying, "One day incels will realize their true strength and numbers, and will overthrow this oppressive feminist system. Start envisioning a world where women fear you."

The fact of the matter is Elliot was not a bad looking young man. He dressed well, came from a good family that had money, and he had a nice car. He also seems to have been quite mentally ill, in a way that may have been diagnosed further down the line had he not succumbed to his dark thoughts. Although he spent a lot of time bemoaning his lack of success with women, it appeared that he never actually asked out a single woman. He just sort of expected all sorts of things to magically happen for him, that women would just fall at his feet.

Would this be a true incel? Or would this be a delusional young man with no grip on reality? The fact that he spent much of his time being positive—he was going to win millions in the lottery—and his total lack of any social connections whatsoever, not just with women, points to the latter.

There have been numerous people who have been designated as incel killers in the years since Elliot Rodger committed mass murder. Chris Harper-Mercer was one of them. On October 15 he killed nine people and injured eight more on the campus of Umpqua Community College, located in Roseburg, Oregon.

Harper-Mercer entered a writing class that he was enrolled in carrying two handguns and fired a warning shot. He first shot a teacher at point-blank range, then began randomly asking students what their religions were telling those that were Christian they would go to Heaven as he shot them. He made a young woman beg for her life before he shot her, and shot another when she tried to talk to him about the consequences of what he was doing.

The police arrived six minutes after the shots started. Harper-Mercer leaned out a window and exchanged gunfire with them. He was hit once in the side, then went back into the classroom and shot himself in the head.

He left a manifesto that mentioned the Isla Vista killings, and how he was mad at the world, in particular he was angry at his lack of having a girlfriend. He had talked of Elliot Rodger in his writing as someone who "stands with the Gods" and had mentioned before on message boards that he was "involuntarily" not having sex.

On the other hand, he doesn't make a single mention of incels in his manifesto, and while he mentions Elliot Rodger, he also writes of numerous other mass shooters including Adam Lanza, and the Columbine killers Eric Harris and Dylan Klebold. He also wrote much of his admiration for Ted Bundy. It appears that while he might have had some admiration for Elliot's acts, he pretty much admired anyone who slaughtered people, no matter what the reason.

Sheldon Bentley was a security guard at a grocery store in Edmonton, Alberta, when he encountered a 51-year-old homeless man named Donald Doucette passed out in an alley. Bentley stomped on his stomach and robbed him of $20 and went back in the store to work. Doucette died almost immediately from massive internal bleeding.

While on trial, Bentley said he was under stress because he hated his job and had been an incel for four years, which lead to him acting so poorly. He was convicted of manslaughter and sentenced to four years in prison.

While it's possible that being a so-called incel contributed to this crime, part of Bentley's job was dealing with homeless, substance abusers every day, often in a very combative manner. It appears that the cause of his crime was much more likely to be that he just snapped because of a variety of factors and did something horrific rather than being an incel.

In Aztec, New Mexico, December 7, 2017, William Atchison pretended to be a student of Aztec High School and used a handgun to kill two students in a hallway before killing himself. Atchison had previously praised Elliot Rodger as "the supreme gentleman" online and had gone by the screen name Elliot Rodger on a Minecraft webpage. However, he also went by over 40 other usernames, some of which were "Adam Lanza" and "future mass shooter." He also often made jokes about Columbine. It appears much more likely that his use of Elliot's name was meant to offend than to him having committed this mass shooting because of being an incel. That would appear to be the least of his troubles.

Nikolas Cruz was the perpetrator of the Parkland, Florida, high school shootings that occurred on February 14, 2018. He killed 17 people and injured seventeen more before he was arrested. He walked into a building, set off a fire alarm, and then started shooting with an AR-15 style automatic rifle at everything that moved for about six minutes before he left the scene and went to a mall and bought a soda. He was eventually arrested about 40 minutes later.

While Cruz had previously posted online "Elliot Rodger will not be forgotten," he had a myriad of issues. He had learning disabilities and emotional issues, to the extent that psychiatrists had suggested he be involuntarily committed in 2013. He also had made online posts where he cut his arms and said that he wanted to die in a gunfight. Once again, it seems like being an incel is a rather small amount of the equation.

On April 23, 2018, in Toronto, Alek Minassian killed 10 people and injured 14 others by hitting pedestrians with a rented van before he was arrested seven minutes after the attacks began. Minassian definitely fits the incel prototype, at least outwardly, posting online before the attack: "Private (Recruit) Minassian Infantry 00010, wishing to speak to Sgt 4chan please. C23249161. The Incel Rebellion has already begun! We will overthrow all the Chads and Stacys! All hail the Supreme Gentleman Elliot Rodger!"

Minassian's family has reported that Minassian had either Asperger's syndrome or autism.

Peter Rodger was quoted as saying about this: "It's not only devastating for the victims [in Toronto], it's also devastating for Elliot's victims, to bring this all up again and make a hero out of a very disturbed individual."

On November 2, 2018, Scott Beierle shot two women and injured four women and a man before killing himself in a shooting at the Hot Yoga Tallahassee studio in Tallahassee, Florida. He had a history of arrests for grabbing women's buttocks and had done it numerous times without being arrested. In 2014 he posted several YouTube videos of himself expressing extreme hatred for women. He expressed anger over not having a girlfriend, mentioning Elliot Rodger in one video. Beierle said he wanted to send a message to young men who are in "the disposition of Elliot Rodger, of not getting any, no love, no nothing."

On Wikipedia, the motive for Scott's crime is written as "incel ideology and misogyny." This does once again bring up the "situation vs. movement" aspect of things. Not every incel has an ideology that suggests slaughtering women.

In January 2019, Christopher Cleary was arrested for posting on Facebook about how he was "planning on shooting up a public place soon and being the next mass shooter" and "killing as many girls as I see" because he had never had a girlfriend and was a virgin. He has been described as an incel in the media. Cleary had a troubled childhood and has been diagnosed with major depressive disorder.

He wrote on Facebook:

> All I wanted was a girlfriend, not 1000 not a bunch of hoes not money none of that. All I wanted was to be loved, yet no one cares about me I'm 27 years old and I've never had a girlfriend before and I'm still a virgin, this is why I'm planning on shooting up a public place soon and being the next mass shooter cause I'm ready to die and all the girls the (sic) turned me down is going to make it right by killing as many girls as I see.

Once again Cleary did not actually follow through on this act.

On June 17, 2019, Bryan Isaack Clyde began what was intended to be a mass shooting at the Earle Cabell Federal Building and Courthouse in Dallas, Texas, but officers from the Federal Protective Service shot and fatally wounded him before he was able to injure anyone. Clyde had shared incel memes on his social media accounts, along with other posts referencing right-wing beliefs and conspiracy theories.

Then of course there is George Sodini, who actually predated Elliot Rodger when it came to what has become known as incel attacks. In fact, he is known in incel communities as the "OG incel. Sodini kept a blog where he wrote of his depression and also talked of his plans for murder, even though he kept in his words "chickening out." Then, on August 4, 2009, in Collier Township, Pennsylvania, he walked into a dance class, shot and killed three women, then killed himself.

Sodini wrote on his website about his rejections by women and his sexual frustration. Some sample entries were: "Thirty million is my rough guesstimate of how many desirable single women there are. A man needs a woman for confidence. He gets a boost on the job, career, with other men, and everywhere else when he knows inside he has someone to spend the night with and who is also a friend. This type of life I see is a closed world with me specifically and totally excluded. Every other guy does this successfully to a degree."

He also wrote on his blog: "Who knows why? I am not ugly or too weird. No sex since July 1990 either (I was 29)" And "Last time I slept all night with a girlfriend it was 1982. Girls and women don't even give me a second look ANYWHERE. Women just don't like me. There are 30 million desirable women in the US (my estimate) and I cannot find one."

Of all the killers on this list, Sodini was by far most like Elliot Rodger, but he certainly wasn't influenced by him.

I wrote this book in large part because I was very surprised to learn no one had ever written a book on Elliot Rodger before. It was even more surprising after reading his so-called manifesto *My Twisted World*. Rarely, if ever, have I read anything that was both so filled with minutia of a lonely day-to-day life, and complete insanity. Elliot Rodger literally had no ability for self-reflection at all, yet he is able to capture his life, and how it unraveled, in a way that's crystal clear.

How did Elliot Rodger become the person he was, and how did he turn from a shy, timid boy to a brutal killer? I'm still not sure I know. Often people say things that seem rather insane, but Elliot truly believed women should be slaughtered because they wouldn't have sex with him, then he actually went out and slaughtered them. He literally thought a perfect world is one where women are rounded up into concentration camps and killed. All while thinking of himself as a supreme gentleman and wondering why women didn't want to hang out with him.

The most fascinating aspect of Elliot was his complete lack of self-awareness. He despised women who he felt weren't attracted to him, yet mocked his roommate for having sex with a girl who is chubby. He felt intense anger towards males who were above him in the social stratus, but was brutally mean to those who he thought were below him.

From a very young age, Elliot had no desire except to be cool and to have sex. First he bleached his hair blonde and tried to become good at skateboarding. Later he bought fancy clothes, and thought his BMW would give him the ticket to coolness and sex. Near the end he became obsessed with winning the lottery, thinking if he only did that, then he could be rich, which of course would get him a wonderful girlfriend, and he wouldn't have to kill anyone.

Never, not once, did he express any desire in his entire manifesto to grow as a person, or to maybe just find a girlfriend he likes that he might have had a good time hanging out with.

What struck me the most while writing this book is how often Elliot would just break down and cry, or scream, and yet no one seemed to notice. A killer was planning a massacre, and all anyone saw was a very shy and awkward young man.

There is no doubt Elliot Rodger was mentally ill, although as a rule I don't like to use that term. But even for someone as depressed, timid, and anxious as he was, it's still unique to see this utter fixation on just one issue for pretty much his entire life from age 12 or so until his death.

People want to blame the Isla Vista killings on Elliot being an incel, or him being mentally ill, or that he had undiagnosed autism. They want to say his parents should have done something or the police should have done something when they visited him after seeing his videos. Maybe James should have told someone his friend Elliot kept talking about flaying women's skin off and boiling them in oil. But why would he? It was just timid little Elliot after all. Maybe it's society's fault. Elliot was obsessed with beauty, riches, and expensive things. Was he just made into who he was because of the society he lived in?

And this is exactly what makes Elliot Rodger so amazing. It's literally impossible to truly know what was going on with him. There has never been a killer quite like Elliot, although George Sodini and Alek Minassian might come close. But neither of them was the Supreme Gentleman. Saint Elliot.

> *I am not part of the human race. Humanity has rejected me. The females of the human species have never wanted to mate with me, so how could I possibly consider myself part of humanity? Humanity has never accepted me among them, and now I know why. I am more than human. I am superior to them all. I am Elliot Rodger... Magnificent, glorious, supreme, eminent... Divine! I am the closest thing there is to a living god. Humanity is a disgusting, depraved, and evil species. It is my purpose to punish them all. I will purify the world of everything that is wrong with it. On the Day of Retribution, I will truly be a powerful god, punishing everyone I deem to be impure and depraved.*

SOURCES:

My Twisted World by Elliot Rodger

Santa Barbara County Sherriff's Office Isla Vista Mass Murder Investigative Summary

Santa Barbara District Attorney Report on the Officer Involved Shooting of Elliot Rodger

Santa Barbara County Sherriff's Report No. 13-10081 (Report on Incident at the House Party)

Southern Poverty Law Center

Texas Domestic Terrorism Threat, 2020

For More News About Brian Whitney,
Signup For Our Newsletter:

http://wbp.bz/newsletter

Word-of-mouth is critical to an author's long-term success. If you appreciated this book please leave a review on the Amazon sales page:

http://wbp.bz/supremegentlemana

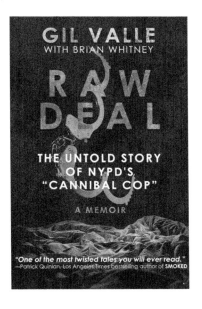

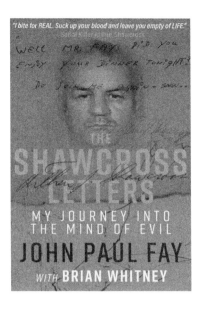

More True Crime You'll Love From WildBlue Press

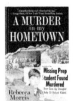

A MURDER IN MY HOMETOWN by Rebecca Morris

Nearly 50 years after the murder of seventeen year old Dick Kitchel, Rebecca Morris returned to her hometown to write about how the murder changed a town, a school, and the lives of his friends.

wbp.bz/hometowna

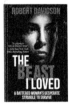

THE BEAST I LOVED by Robert Davidson

Robert Davidson again demonstrates that he is a master of psychological horror in this riveting and hypnotic story ... I was so enthralled that I finished the book in a single sitting. "—James Byron Huggins, International Bestselling Author of The Reckoning

wbp.bz/tbila

BULLIED TO DEATH by Judith A. Yates

On September 5, 2015, in a public park in LaVergne, Tennessee, fourteen-year-old Sherokee Harriman drove a kitchen knife into her stomach as other teens watched in horror. Despite attempts to save her, the girl died, and the coroner ruled it a "suicide." But was it? Or was it a crime perpetuated by other teens who had bullied her?

wbp.bz/btda

SUMMARY EXECUTION by Michael Withey

"An incredible true story that reads like an international crime thriller peopled with assassins, political activists, shady FBI informants, murdered witnesses, a tenacious attorney, and a murderous foreign dictator."—Steve Jackson, New York Times bestselling author of NO STONE UNTURNED

wbp.bz/sea

Printed in Great Britain
by Amazon